Business Guides on the Go

"Business Guides on the Go" presents cutting-edge insights from practice on particular topics within the fields of business, management, and finance. Written by practitioners and experts in a concise and accessible form the series provides professionals with a general understanding and a first practical approach to latest developments in business strategy, leadership, operations, HR management, innovation and technology management, marketing or digitalization. Students of business administration or management will also benefit from these practical guides for their future occupation/careers.

These Guides suit the needs of today's fast reader.

Michael S. Tomczyk

Neo-Innovation

Ideas, Insights, and Tools to Compete in a New Era

 Springer

Michael S. Tomczyk
Collegeville, PA, USA

ISSN 2731-4758   ISSN 2731-4766   (electronic)
Business Guides on the Go
ISBN 978-3-031-74302-3   ISBN 978-3-031-74303-0   (eBook)
https://doi.org/10.1007/978-3-031-74303-0

This Springer imprint is published by the registered company Springer Nature Switzerland AG
The registered company address is: Gewerbestrasse 11, 6330 Cham, Switzerland

If disposing of this product, please recycle the paper.

Why You Need This Book

We are standing at the dawn of a new era of civilization which we can call the NeoWorld. The NeoWorld has forced us to adopt new ways of doing business, new management styles and new forms of innovation which we can call "Neo-Innovation."

This new era has imposed radical changes in where we work, how we meet and communicate, where we get food and entertainment, and much more. For business leaders, entrepreneurs, and innovators, this new era has created a host of challenges and has also given us exciting opportunities to re-define the world and re-invent the future.

Whether you are in a company, government agency, in school, or starting an entrepreneurial venture, you need to understand how Neo-Innovation is changing how we solve problems, generate new ideas, and create the future.

This book is designed to inspire and guide you as you think about and work to develop any creative idea or project. These frameworks and examples can be applied to any area where new approaches are needed to break outdated rules, dissolve boundaries, and turn problems into opportunities.

Sometimes it seems like innovation is a business concept, but innovation is not limited to business and science, especially in the NeoWorld. The principles and tools of Neo-Innovation can be applied to any aspect of your life, home, school, social groups, lifestyle, and more.

To practice Neo-Innovation, think about new problems and future problems that need to be solved, and new opportunities that can be exploited. This includes problems and opportunities that most people may not be aware of yet. To get started, you will need to think outside the box. Be creative. Pick a goal, figure out how to get there, then go for it. Make progress every day. Invite your colleagues, friends, and family to motivate you. When you accomplish one goal, choose another. Keep going. Have fun. Neo-Innovation is a lifelong undertaking and a source of never-ending joy.

As you read this book, please think about how these ideas relate to your life, your job, and your future. Hopefully the insights presented here will help you navigate the NeoWorld to compete, survive, and succeed.

Acknowledgments

I want to thank the many friends and colleagues in many countries who have supported my innovation career over the years, including business leaders, scientists, engineers, and marketeers who contributed time, talent, and ideas.

I want to thank Stan Kasper, Saiful Khandaker, Justin Shi, Rabiul Kareem, and a legion of friends and fans in the Commodore community. I am especially grateful to the many academic colleagues and industry partners I was privileged to work with at the Wharton School, Drexel, Temple, Villanova, and other business schools.

Many of the innovations described in this book were pioneered and developed by personal friends and colleagues in science, medicine, and industry—special thanks to these Neo-Innovators for the examples and images they provided, which I am delighted to include and acknowledge.

Most important, I am grateful to the global innovation community including students, teachers, entrepreneurs, scientists, engineers, and business leaders in many countries who keep alive the spirit of innovation.

Contents

About the Author

Michael S. Tomczyk is an innovator, entrepreneur, futurist, and an expert on radical/disruptive innovation.

As a technology pioneer, he is best known for his role in the development and launch of the first home computers at Commodore in the 1980s which jump-started the home computer revolution. He was product manager for the VIC-20 which was the first computer to sell one million units and co-designed the first million-seller modem (VICModem). He has been called the "marketing father" of the home computer.

As a corporate executive, consultant, and product manager, Michael has been involved in several world-changing innovations including biosciences, ecommerce, gene therapy, nanotechnology, and most recently Fintech and Blockchain. He is a founding board member of Fintech Ecosystems Development Corporation (NASDAQ: FEXD) and co-founder of a private blockchain venture (SMC Lab).

Michael has written more than 150 articles, as well as newspaper and magazine columns. His books and reports include *The Home Computer Wars, The Future of Biosciences*, and *Nano-innovation: What Every Manager Needs to Know*. He has contributed chapters to several books including *After Shock: The World's Foremost Futurists Reflect on 50 Years of Future Shock* (2020).

In addition to practicing innovation, he has also studied and developed new innovation strategies and tactics. For 18 years, he served as Managing Director of innovation research initiatives at the prestigious Wharton School. At Wharton, he worked with core faculty to launch and manage the Emerging Technologies Management Research Program, Mack Center for Technological Innovation, and Mack Institute for Innovation Management (a $50 Million research institute). He also served on the Advanced Computing advisory group at Temple University and was Innovator in Residence at Villanova University.

Michael holds a Master's Degree in Environmental Studies (MES) from the University of Pennsylvania, a Master of Business Administration (MBA) from UCLA, and a BA in Literature and Journalism from the University of Wisconsin-Oshkosh.

He was a captain in the U.S. Army where he was Information Officer for the XVIII Airborne Corps at Ft. Bragg; Information Officer at the 1st Signal Brigade in Vietnam; and USASTRATCOM/United Nations Command in South Korea. He experienced combat in Vietnam where he was awarded the Bronze Star and Arny Commendation Medal.

Part I

Welcome to the NeoWorld

I read Alice in Wonderland and Through the Looking Glass when I was in second grade. For me, the most memorable scene was Alice running beside the Red Queen, out of breath and racing to keep up, when the Red Queen turns to her and says, "Here it takes all the running you can do, to keep in the same place. If you want to get somewhere else, you must run at least twice as fast as that!"

This was true in Wonderland, and today it's true for innovators racing to keep up and move forward in the NeoWorld.

1

The NeoWorld Is Different, Unique, and Surreal

Most of us grew up and developed our careers in a world that is much different from today. Our world was more familiar. It changed more slowly. There were rules and boundaries that were easy to understand that we could comfortably rely on.

In the old world, when we thought about something "new," we mostly thought about new cars, or new movies and TV shows, or maybe something new on the menu of our favorite restaurant, or some new gizmo or gadget we saw online.

Then suddenly we were shocked out of our comfort zones by a global pandemic that transformed the lives of everyone on the planet.

Almost overnight, the world was transformed into something alien, bizarre, and unfamiliar. It seemed like almost everything was morphing into new forms. We had to change how we work, play, communicate, dine, and shop. We had to learn new ways to manage our lives, our careers, our social relationships, and more.

A new era of civilization was being created, an extraordinary new world—a *NeoWorld*.

This new world is dangerous and scary but also promising and intriguing. It is fraught with new problems and challenges we've never experienced before. The NeoWorld has also opened the way to exciting new opportunities in business, science, and social media. It has created new innovation ecosystems that are transforming civilization and humanity.

The COVID pandemic is credited with a fundamental transformation of the digital infrastructure of business, according to numerous articles and reports. Many prestigious research and consulting organizations have confirmed how technologies, applications, and industries and markets have been transformed by the pandemic. Articles, reports, and surveys on this topic have been published by McKinsey, Pew Research Center, LinkedIn, and *Forbes* to name a few.

As a 2021 McKinsey global survey observed: "In just a few months' time, the COVID-19 crisis has brought about years of change in the way companies in all sectors and regions do business."[1]

Before the COVID pandemic, our world consisted of communities, companies, countries, and cultures. Today the world has evolved into a matrix of ecosystems and mini-ecosystems, where everyone and everything are connected.

To manage all the changes brought to us by the NeoWorld, we have had to become NeoManagers, which means we need to master new skills and strategies. We have to rethink the future—the NeoFuture—so we can anticipate and solve unexpected problems lurking on the near horizon. We need to find creative ways to profit from new possibilities. We need to become Neo-Innovators.

This book is intended to give you a sense of what it means to be a Neo-Innovator, a NeoManager, and a NeoFuturist, so you can successfully navigate the NeoWorld.

---

[1] McKinsey & Company; How COVID-19 had pushed companies over the technology tipping point—and transformed business forever; McKinsey Survey; 5 October 2020.

The NeoWorld Was Spawned by COVID

It's not often that we can pinpoint when a new era is born, like the Space Age or the Internet Age, but we can pretty much agree that January 2020 is a good starting point for the birth of the current era, which we call the NeoWorld. This is when the worldwide pandemic gained momentum and forced people in all industries and markets to make radical adjustments to their policies, work routines, and core operations and created new challenges and opportunities for innovators. The NeoWorld required many disruptive and radical innovations and forced professional innovators to change how they approach the development of new technologies and applications—which is the focus of this book.

COVID-19 was a lethal form of the coronavirus that emerged in Fall 2019 and quickly became the most serious infectious disease to threaten the world in over a century. By January 2020 the pandemic caused so many changes that we can legitimately say that COVID ushered in a new era of civilization.

When the coronavirus pandemic first appeared, it was like living in a zombie apocalypse. It was so surreal. Infected people weren't trying to bite (or eat) us, but we could catch a fatal disease if someone who was infected coughed or sneezed near us or if we touched something that was touched by a COVID victim.

Since COVID was technically incurable and there were no vaccines at first, the best thing we could do was try to avoid catching the virus. Lots of changes were imposed. We had to wear masks and gloves and avoid crowded places. Supermarkets required shoppers to wear masks and established special hours for senior citizens and other high-risk customers (see Fig. 1.1). Movie theatres, restaurants, and office buildings were closed for half a year or more. Whole cities were quarantined. Air travel was restricted. Schools were closed. Instead of meeting or greeting someone with a handshake, we started fist bumping.

If we contracted the virus, we could wind up in intensive care on a ventilator, but there weren't enough ventilators to treat everyone. More than 6 million people died in the first 2 years, and by 2023 as many as 15 million deaths were attributed to the pandemic. By comparison, the

Fig. 1.1 During the pandemic, the author (*shown here*) was one of millions of shoppers forced to wear masks in supermarkets. Many supermarkets established special shopping for high-risk shoppers, as shown on this sign at a Redner's super-market in Pennsylvania. (Photo by M. Tomczyk)

Spanish flu that struck the world a century ago in 1918 killed between 30 and 100 million people. The COVID-19 pandemic was the most serious pandemic since the Spanish flu.

Luckily, we live in a world where high-tech innovation—including medical innovation—has become one of our key competencies as a society. As soon as COVID began to spread, medical innovators rushed to develop vaccines which normally took years to develop and test. The first COVID vaccines and boosters were ready in only 6 months which was a remarkable achievement.

Nevertheless, even the best COVID vaccines didn't always work, and many large groups remained at risk because of their age, health, or jobs. Virtually every nation in the world was forced to adopt lockdowns, shut-downs, and quarantines because the only surefire way to minimize the spread of COVID was to keep people separated and minimize human contact.

The result was the equivalent of a tsunami that swept away whole industries and forever transformed how we work, connect, communicate, socialize, shop, learn, and entertain ourselves. No one was prepared for all the changes. There were so many twists and turns that we could hardly keep pace.

The post-pandemic world is still evolving. We continue to need new forms of innovation and management to cope with changes that are governing our daily lives, influencing our behavior, and redefining the future. The most normal day-to-day functions like shopping, holding a business meeting, or chatting with friends have morphed into entirely new forms. We're still experimenting and changing how we work, meet, and communicate and even how we shop for clothes, socialize, watch TV, and share messages.

This new era has given us a different kind of world, but that doesn't mean it's a safer world. The world continues to be shaped by climate change, natural disasters, military conflicts, and social trends. All of these phenomena, which used to be hidden from sight or reported in newscasts and sound bites, are now reported in real time. Our access to all kinds of information is unprecedented. It's been said that information is power, but in the new era, information is part of our cultural DNA.

Because we're all connected via social media and able to capture and share videos on our smartphones, everything that is happening in the world is visible. We can watch detailed news reports about anything, anywhere, including news that used to be objective and now is often biased (and sometimes fake). We can see earthquakes, floods, wildfires, and tsunamis in real time. We can see wars being fought. We can binge-watch a whole season of TV shows in one weekend, including excellent series from Korea, India, and many other countries which has broadened our international awareness. When a new product is launched, we see it immediately in pop-up ads on social media and search engines.

Being able to see problems in real time means we can start solving these problems faster. New technologies and applications are also available faster, and that means we are constantly getting new tools to help make the world a better place.

What's Neo About the NeoWorld? I often say that the new world feels surreal, but in truth, the NeoWorld is real...*very* real. Many things in the world that used to be considered far-out or surreal are now part of the new normal.

For example, we've been able to study atoms and molecules for more than a century, but being able to manipulate atoms was an elusive goal. Androids have been part of our popular culture since Isaac Asimov popularized robots with his robot stories in the 1930s, but now robotic engineers are creating humanoid robots that look and talk like their inventors. Sending nanobots into the bloodstream like a scene from an *Ant-Man* movie was the stuff of fiction, but now it's a scientific possibility. What used to be surreal is now becoming real, and it's happening fast.

Think about all the changes that have occurred in the past few years and changes that are underway right now. Smart machines, self-driving cars, digital people, humanoid robots, and colonies on Mars are no longer science fiction. They still sound surreal when we describe them, but in the NeoWorld they have become real possibilities that Neo-Innovators can actually achieve.

Being alert to new changes and monitoring their impact will help you become a better Neo-Innovator, whether you use what you learn in your job, in your personal life, or in some way in a social application that helps other people.

I invite you to join me in exploring the significance of these changes, to better understand what's needed, what's possible, and what's coming next.

2

What It Means to Be Neo

Neo is a Greek prefix that means "new." Most of us can name several words that begin with neo. For example, neoclassic, neoprene, neoconservative, neolithic, neologic, neophyte, neonatal, neorealism, and trivia fans will note that Neo is the name of Keanu Reeves' character in the iconic *Matrix* movies. Neo is used to describe anything that is undergoing some sort of radical change, disruption, and reinvention.

In the business world we are seeing neo-industries that didn't exist before or are just beginning to take off after years of false starts and missteps. Think about autonomous vehicles, airborne drones, humanoid robots, and new forms of artificial intelligence like ChatGPT. These are all Neo-Innovations that caused us to radically alter our behavior and use new ways of doing things.

To better understand the concept, try attaching the prefix "neo" to almost anything, and then ask yourself, how is the *Neo* version different or unique compared to the old version? How does the *Neo* version cause us to change our behavior and do things differently? This is how radical innovations are created, and in the NeoWorld, it's easy to find examples of how this works.

M. S. Tomczyk, *Neo-Innovation*, Business Guides on the Go,
https://doi.org/10.1007/978-3-031-74303-0_2

Neo-Marketing During my career, I specialized mostly in marketing which includes advertising, public relations, and product development. In the NeoWorld, most aspects of marketing have changed dramatically. The last generation grew up reading print ads and watching TV commercials.

The generation that is coming of age in the NeoWorld spends much of the day online and can't avoid seeing pop-up ads in applications, websites, search engines, and social media. Pop-ups are customized to our interests and needs because search engines, shopping sites, and social media track our online choices, what we search for, and even how long we linger on a screen. These behaviors are turned into personalized ads that get pushed to our laptop and smartphone screens. To some this may seem intrusive, but most of us appreciate personalized ads because they save us time and money, too, for example, by alerting us when things we like come on sale.

Neo-Dating If we combine Neo and dating, we get Neo-Dating—creative ways to meet new friends and find dating partners. How we meet people has changed a lot and continues to evolve in the NeoWorld.

When COVID closed bars, concerts, and social gatherings, it became harder for singles, divorcees, widows, and widowers to meet and socialize. Many people started using online dating sites to post preferences, profiles, and pictures. This actually turned out to be a better way to meet people than hanging out in bars and nightclubs. What if you don't drink? What if your perfect match stayed home the night you visited a bar, and you never even got a chance to meet her (or him)? In the old dating world, so much was left to chance encounters. In the NeoWorld, dating became more efficient. Online dating sites became the equivalent of romantic search engines.

Of course, searching online for someone who might be fun to date or a potential life partner is not like shopping online for clothes at Macy's. Online daters have to be careful to avoid catfishers who create false identities and grifters trying to steal personal information or get money. Nevertheless, by 2023 there were more than 1500 online dating sites and applications worldwide, with names like eHarmony, Match.com, Tinder, and Zoosk. According to Statistica, online dating providers were projected to reach 441 million active users by the end of 2023.

Neo-Medicine Neo-Medicine includes a vast array of new medical techniques made possible by emerging technologies, medical research, and clinical trials. Most have not yet been fully standardized or commercialized. There are many medical Neo-Innovations that are still mostly early stage and not fully developed such as gene editing, but they are exciting because they give hope to millions of disease victims throughout the world. More information is included in Part IV (NeoTrends).

Neo-Money (Cryptocurrency) A decade ago if someone said we're going to create new forms of money, we would assume they were talking about redesigning paper bills and coins, to replace old designs and prevent counterfeiting. We wouldn't have predicted the rise of cryptocurrencies.

The first cryptocurrency, called Bitcoin, was introduced in 2009 by an anonymous innovator as an alternative to traditional banking. Other cryptos which are often referred to generically as "bitcoins," include: Ethereum, Cardano, Dogecoin, and Solana.

Bitcoin and other cryptos use a distributed ledger/recordkeeping technology called blockchain to encrypt and record transactions in a shared database network. When bitcoin was first introduced, each coin was valued at a fraction of a penny. Millions of people started trading and "mining" bitcoins.

Cryptocurrencies range in value from a fraction of a penny to tens of thousands of dollars. In 2022, the value of a bitcoin peaked at $61,000 for each coin. On October 1, 2023, a bitcoin was valued at $26,000. Today, there are currently approximately 23,000 cryptocurrencies in the NeoWorld. By comparison, there are only about 200 traditional government-backed ("fiat") currencies.

Neobanking/Fintechs When the pandemic forced lockdowns of public places in 2020, many people stopped visiting physical bank branches to avoid standing in lines at teller windows. Customers and store clerks were discouraged from handling paper bills and coins. This opened the way for financial service providers called fintechs to provide online banking services that are cheaper and faster than traditional banks. There are more than 25,000 fintech service providers in the world, with almost half based in the United States.

Fintechs typically do not have physical offices or branches. The goal of most fintechs is to improve and automate financial services to help companies and consumers achieve their goals.

For example, migrant workers can use fintech apps on their smartphones to send money home to families in their home countries faster and cheaper than banks and money transfer services. Many unbanked customers live in remote areas of the world that don't have physical bank branches. Unbanked customers can use their smartphones to access banking services. Another fintech example is P2P lending, where members of a network loan money to each other instead of borrowing from a bank or loan company.

Neo-Cities—also called smart cities—feature energy-neutral "net zero" buildings that produce as much energy as they use. Some cities are reengineering traffic lights by adding wireless sensors that help autonomous/self-driving vehicles navigate city streets and creating smart highways with sensors embedded in the road. A future version of Neo-Cities involves building floating cities in coastal locations that are expected to be flooded by rising sea levels.

In many cities, CCTV cameras keep communities under constant surveillance—which was originally depicted as a "nightmare scenario" by George Orwell in his 1949 dystopian book *Nineteen Eighty Four*. Today the need for crime prevention has made video surveillance acceptable and desirable. We even allow *Big Brother*-style search engines, advertisers, and AI chatbots to monitor our Internet clicks and customize pop up ads, news, and other content.

Neo-Work has revolutionized how people do their jobs, with more people working at home and holding meetings online instead of in physical conference rooms. When the pandemic shut down companies and office buildings, many of us started working at home, which saved gas, commuting time, and physical office costs. After the pandemic subsided, many organizations realized that telework was more efficient and kept work-at-home practices in place, for all or part of the work week. Being able to meet anywhere anytime online also means that organizations can tap the smartest, most creative (and affordable) programmers, engineers, editors, and other professionals wherever they are located, in the world. This also gives new opportunities to skilled workers in developing countries who otherwise might not have a chance to work for global enterprises.

Neo-Shopping means we can go online to buy almost anything from anywhere in the world and have it delivered to our door, at the best available price, instead of traveling to retail stores. We can use our smartphone to order something from China or India and have it delivered half way around the world to our house or apartment.

When department stores were forced to close during the pandemic, the resulting surge in home shopping made shopping sites like Amazon and Alibaba the largest retail organizations in the world. The "supply chain" from order to warehouse to delivery service to truck to doorstep was totally automated. Many shoppers started using their smartphones to buy merchandise which was like carrying a whole department store or product catalog in your pocket. Some retailers like Macys made a smooth transition to online sales and supplemented home delivery with in-store pickup as an option. Most restaurants forced to close their dining rooms during the pandemic added home delivery and pickup services.

Neo-Human sounds like a concept from science fiction—which it is—but the science reality is that we are gaining the ability to genetically engineer the human species. In theory we can use gene editing to create disease resistant babies, as well as genetically enhanced athletes, soldiers, and workers.

The term "Neo-Human" describes a new generation of human beings with enhanced abilities and special powers. The term was originally coined by genetics pioneer Dr. Odell Harrison. A Neo-Human could be a person born with a gene that conveys a special trait such as the potential to live past 100, or it could be a person who is genetically engineered with special attributes or "powers." It also could be someone enhanced in some way by technology such as cyborgs which in science fiction are bionic humans with both organic and electromechanical body parts.

Elon Musk has joked that we are so well integrated with our smartphones and computers that we already are cyborgs. Professor Yuval Harari at the Hebrew University of Jerusalem believes we will be able to "upgrade" ourselves by merging with machines to become cyborgs in 200 years, but only wealthy people may be able to afford it.[1]

In the field of innovation, there is a concept called *Transhumanism* that promotes the belief that emerging technologies can be used to symbiotically enhance human capabilities and create new versions of human beings called *posthumans*. Ray Kurzweil has predicted that humans will one day "transcend biology."

In terms of creating Neo-Humans, which would be an extraordinary Neo-Innovation, medical researchers are currently studying which lifestyles and genes allow people to become centenarians (living past 100) or supercentenarians (living past 110). Northwestern University has conducted fascinating research on people they call *superagers* who are men and women in their 80 s who have the mental acuity of people in their 50s.[2] Other researchers have begun to identify genes associated with longevity, which theoretically could be transferred to people who want to live longer, using gene editing.

Neo-War refers to new types of weapons, especially GPS-guided drones used in the Ukraine-Russia and Israel-Hamas wars. These drones are equipped with video cameras to help drone operators identify and paint targets for smart artillery. Drones have replaced human forward observers previously used to identify artillery targets. A future worry for military planners is the use of swarms of drones to overwhelm antimissile systems protecting a military facility, warship, or city.

One of the most disturbing developments in the NeoWorld has been the use of aerial drones by regional powers and terrorist groups to harass and attack civilian commercial ships. This is an entirely new form of international piracy.

Neo-War innovations have also included some ultrasophisticated defensive weapons. The best known defensive innovations include the American Patriot antimissile system and Israel's Iron Dome antimissile umbrella and Iron Beam laser defense system. American and NATO

---

[1] Oakes, Troy; Will Wealthy People Become Cyborgs in the Next 200 Years?; Science; 17 September 2021.

[2] LaMotte, Study finds more clues as to why "SuperAgers" have better brains; CNN Health; 13 July 2023.

warships have successfully intercepted and stopped missiles fired at ships in the Red Sea.

However, firing missiles to intercept incoming rockets is expensive. More cost-effective antimissile systems are needed, which offers challenges and opportunities for military innovators. For example, Israel's Iron Dome antimissile system costs as much as $50,000 for each defensive missile! In contrast, Israel's Iron Beam laser costs only $3.50 per shot, so if Iron Beam proves effective, it would offer a major value proposition.

Neo Is Ubiquitous These examples of *Neo* innovations illustrate how much the world has changed and why it really is a NeoWorld, not just for innovators but for everyone, everywhere.

What other *Neo* examples can you think of? Anything that combines "Neo" with something that exists today is a potential idea for any radical innovation that could change the world.

Quick...Create Something Neo!

If you want to feel what it's like to create something *Neo*, try this simple exercise:

1. **Create a *Neo* concept**—pick something you're familiar with, interested in, or curious about, like NeoCooking, NeoSports, or NeoSchool.
2. **Now, describe what this *Neo*-something might be.** How would it change our behavior? What new benefits would it bring us? What problems or challenges might result? How might this *Neo*-something evolve in the next few years or decades? How could it impact the future, for better or for worse. Search online to see if someone is working on this now. Think about how you might participate and contribute.
3. **Study what pioneers and entrepreneurs are doing in this area.** Check out "what's possible" that some innovators are working on now. You can find almost anything online today, which includes early stage technologies and applications that entrepreneurs are developing.

4. **Think about how you might participate in helping to make them happen.** Do you want to take classes or workshops to learn more about a particular area that is ripe for innovation? Look for companies that are developing technologies or applications that could change the world that you'd like to be involved in. If you're really interested, you can apply for a job.

When it comes to innovation, there are many ways to participate. The first rule of innovation is there are no rules. So if you're interested in something that's really *Neo*, find a way to get involved and good luck!

Part II

Neo-Innovation

In 1994 I joined the Wharton School as managing director of the Emerging Technologies Research Program. On my first day I was standing in the hallway with Professor Sid Winter, who was discussing a business concept with another faculty member. To show that I understood what they were discussing, I said, "That's a really good business model."

Sid turned to me and said, "Michael, that's not a business model."

"So what is it?" I asked, suddenly humbled.

"That's a sensemaking framework," Sid replied.

From that moment on, sensemaking frameworks became part of my innovation DNA. During my two decades in academia, the most valuable skill I learned was how to develop and apply sensemaking frameworks to complex situations and tasks.

3

Making Sense of Innovation

In this chapter we'll explore the various types of innovation and offer some sensemaking frameworks to help you understand and apply innovation strategies in the NeoWorld.

We all need to understand innovation because innovation is the engine that drives civilization forward. New technologies, applications, systems, and processes are essential to our success and survival, wherever we live in the world. Innovations drive economic growth and profitability. They create new markets, make our lives easier and more productive, and provide novel solutions to all kinds of problems.

How many innovations can you list right now, off the top of your head?

Here's a quick list: age-slowing drugs, autonomous vehicles, blockchain, chatbots, cryptocurrencies, generative AI (ChatGPT), gene editing, humanoid robots, the metaverse, nanomaterials, net zero buildings, nuclear fusion, quantum computers, self-driving vehicles, video doorbells, and Web 3.0, to name a few.

© The Author(s), under exclusive license to Springer Nature Switzerland AG 2024
M. S. Tomczyk, *Neo-Innovation*, Business Guides on the Go,
https://doi.org/10.1007/978-3-031-74303-0_3

Innovation Comes in Many Forms

There are several different kinds of innovation. Here are some useful definitions, starting with the basic types of innovation that most managers and marketeers use today:

Innovation is the *implementation* of a new idea, discovery, or invention, to *create value*. This is a practical business-oriented definition that links innovation to commercial or social value. Innovations are mostly used to solve problems and create opportunities.

Please note that the value of an innovation isn't limited to financial profits. Value can also include social value. Finding new ways to improve the world is often more important than making money.

Also, there is a difference between an invention and an innovation. An innovation is the *implementation* of an invention—however, many inventions are never actually built or commercialized. For example, Leonardo Da Vinci sketched a helicopter in the late 1400s so you could say he invented it, but the first working helicopters weren't built and tested until 1905–1910 which is when we can say they became innovations.

Many of the innovations we're most familiar with come from emerging technologies. An *emerging technology is a science-based innovation that has the potential to create a new industry or market.* This definition was developed by our faculty core team while I was managing director of the Emerging Technologies Management Research Program at the Wharton School in the late 1990s.

Emerging technologies often make existing technologies obsolete and often threaten (or destroy) existing industries. How you know whether a platform, technology, or application is a threat or an opportunity depends on your point of view and also your talent. Some innovators have a natural ability to turn threats into opportunities.

* **Incremental innovations are a series of *gradual improvements* to a company's existing products, services, processes, or methods.** Examples include new versions of software that we update periodically or year-to-year changes in new car designs. As many as 90% of all innovations are incremental.

A great example of incremental innovation is a concept called *Kaizen* that was developed in Japan after World War II. Kai means "change," and zen means "for the better," so Kaizen means "change for the better." The best known practitioner of Kaizen is Toyota where employees are encouraged and incentivized to strive for continuous improvement at every worksite. The goal is to impose "continuous change" to maximize quality and productivity, eliminate waste, and increase efficiency.

- **Disruptive innovation is an innovation that creates a new market and/or transforms, threatens, or destroys an existing company, industry, or market.** A good example of a disruptive innovation is the transition from brick and mortar retail stores to click and order applications that allow us to order virtually anything online and have it delivered to our homes and offices. E-commerce was another disruptive innovation. Digital photography and the smartphone camera disrupted the market for traditional film cameras. Other disruptive innovations include digital music (iTunes), streaming media (Netflix), and social media (Facebook, Twitter).

Innovation icon Clayton Christensen and his collaborators coined the phrase "disruptive innovation" in 1995.[1] He wrote that disruptive innovation occurs when (typically) a smaller company enters a market with a new product, service, or business strategy that challenges incumbent businesses including well-entrenched market leaders.

This definition has evolved over the decades, and in the NeoWorld, it is part of the new normal. Today, disruptive innovators can be any size company or even an individual working in a garage or dorm room. Disruptive innovators can beat incumbents by taking existing technologies to other countries and markets where the technology hasn't been introduced yet, such as Mo Ibrahim's introduction of mobile phone networks to sub-Saharan Africa.

Disruptive innovations don't always come from small companies starting "from the bottom" which was Christensen's original concept. Many large corporations have become disruptive innovators, and most of these succeeded because they came from outside the industry of the

---

[1] Christensen, Clayton et al., What Is Disruptive Innovation?; Harvard Business Review; December 2015.

market leaders and blindsided the incumbents. Examples of large corporate disruptors include Amazon which disintermediated bookstores and department stores, Tesla which pioneered electric vehicles, and email giants like Google and AOL which disintermediated snail mail. More recently, chatbots, virtual assistants, and AI apps were mostly commercialized by large corporations such as Alibaba, Amazon, Google, IBM, Meta, and NVIDIA. Generative AI is now an $80 billion industry. Many of the Neo-Innovations described in this book were developed or funded by large corporations and sponsors.

It can be argued that disruptive innovation is more common today because the pace of change has increased dramatically in the NeoWorld. Product life cycles are shorter. Information about emerging technologies is readily available on the Internet. Innovators can start commercializing new scientific discoveries and applications as soon as new science is reported.

Also, despite ubiquitous communication, incumbent corporations still miss emerging technologies and applications until it's too late to adapt and compete. That's because senior managers often have tunnel vision. They fall into a comfort zone because current or legacy products are still generating sales, and other industries may not be on their radar screens which makes it easy to get blindsided. Companies that rely on experienced senior managers and exclude younger employees from product teams may find that they are also excluding the people who are closest to, and understand best, emerging technologies and applications.

- **Radical innovation is an innovation that** *changes the behavior of customers and users* **and creates new markets driven by new patterns of use and consumption.** This is the type of innovation that transforms our lives. A great example of a radical innovation is the smartphone. Think about how smartphones have changed our lives.

Most radical innovations—often called "game-changing" innovations—come from (1) entrepreneurs who launch new ventures to commercialize a new technology or application and (2) large corporations like Google or Tesla that have well-established "cultures of innovation" where constant change is normal and encouraged.

- **Neo-Innovation is a form of radical innovation that includes new approaches to solving problems and creating opportunities in the NeoWorld.** In this new world, which is the beginning of a new era, everything is more open, more global, less secret, and easier to implement and commercialize.

  For example, applications like Zoom and tools like ChatGPT make it easier for everyone in the world to connect, communicate, and collaborate on new ideas and inventions. The result is that we are about to enter an innovation Renaissance where a bold new generation of radical innovations will impact every industry and market. Many of the emerging technologies and applications that are already reshaping the future are described in the last part of this book.

  Neo-Innovation is forcing every organization to get more involved in multicultural management, open communication, active networking and collaboration, multitasking, and fast decision-making. Neo-Innovators view organizations as ecosystems instead of hierarchical entities. They value flexibility over rigidity. They foster and encourage change. They involve everyone inside and outside the company in the innovation process. They are not reluctant to navigate choppy waters. They take risks and break rules.

  Neo-Innovators reward excellence, efficiency, creativity, flexibility, and speed. They focus on trust building and problem-solving. They work across borders and boundaries. They strive to build business families and innovation cultures that are comfortable with complexity, risk-taking, and change.

  They respond quickly to opportunities because in a connected world everyone knows everything, and if they don't jump on an idea, someone else will. They also address problems and deficiencies quickly because they understand that anything negative about a company or its products will be instantly revealed, reported, and discussed.

The Neo-Innovation Landscape

How is Neo-Innovation different or unique?

Before the NeoWorld, innovators relied on proven tried and true methods to create new technologies and products. We used brainstorming sessions and workshops to generate ideas and tested new products in focus groups. We thought in terms of product life cycles and only replaced an existing product if we had to. We focused on threats inside our industry and market and ignored threats that might come from other industries because most competitors in other industries didn't have the knowledge or resources to compete with us.

In past years, we typically introduced a new product in the United States or Europe and then waited until it was well established in the home market before taking it overseas. Often, people in developing countries had to wait years to gain access to the latest computer, smartphone, software, or medical drug. In the NeoWorld, geographic borders and market boundaries have been swept away. The world had become a uni-market, seamless and connected.

If we look at the innovation landscape, we can see some of the impressive changes that are making it easier to innovate across border, industries, and markets.

Ideation Is Borderless The process of generating new ideas, known as "ideation," is easier, faster, and more open than ever before thanks to online apps like Zoom Meetings, Google Meet, Microsoft Teams, Webex, and WhatsApp. Instead of bringing people together at company headquarters, university conference room, or off-site workshop, we can now convene a brainstorming meeting on short notice and get people all over the world to participate in a video session. Ideas can be captured on shared screens, and the results can be sent to other partners and colleagues who couldn't attend the meeting. This is a much more efficient method for developing innovations.

Market Research Is More Virtual If we want to get customer reactions to a new type of video doorbell, we don't have to contact a dozen people and get them to come to an office for a focus group meeting. We don't have to mail or email surveys and wait for the results. We can use personal profiles to target 100 or 1000 qualified customers and invite them to go online to tell us what they like and don't like about a new product or service, to help us optimize the features.

Markets Are Global and Multicultural In the NeoWorld we can buy products and services from anywhere in the world. Digital applications and manuals are typically downloaded instead of delivered on a CD or jump drive packaged in a box. Clothes are shipped directly from companies in China, India, or Vietnam, with payments made via Amazon.com, PayPal, Zelle, or other money transfer providers: UPS, DHL, FedEx, and the post office.

Language Is No Longer a Barrier Today if I want to access a website where products are offered in another country, in a different language, I can ask my search engine to translate the Web page or choose my language on the site. This also means that companies, ventures, and innovation groups can collaborate in different languages to develop new products. This means we can access the most creative people, the best programmers, and collaborators wherever they are, anywhere in the world. In the NeoWorld, language and geography are no longer barriers to global innovation.

There Are No Secrets Scientific research and emerging technologies used to be mostly hidden from view in company and university research labs and kept secret so competitors wouldn't learn about them. Many entrepreneurs worked quietly out of sight in dorm rooms and garages.

In the NeoWorld, search engines give us immediate access to almost all knowledge. It's easier than ever to share new ideas in open innovation communities where everyone is invited to participate. Even secrets are available online. Trade secrets and confidential data are routinely accessed and leaked by hackers. Foreign governments are actively engaged in stealing intellectual property, new product designs, and trade secrets.

Most Neo-Innovations Are Technology and Application Systems Today, most innovations are not stand-alone technologies. They are mostly systems comprised of many different technologies. For example, the next generation of computers, smartphones, video doorbells, and other smart devices are all made possible by *systems* of technologies—hardware, software, firmware, input/output connections and algorithms, wireless connectivity, touchscreens, security safeguards, and, most recently, a new generation of artificial intelligence functions.

Most Innovation Surprises Come from Crossing Industry Boundaries
The landscape of failed industries is littered with the epitaphs of companies that got blindsided by disruptive innovations. Companies are often caught by surprise when an innovation is developed in a different industry because what's happening in other industries and markets is often not on their radar screens.

Who would imagine that digital photography would crush the traditional film photography business or that a few years later, smartphones with built-in cameras would disrupt the digital camera industry? Who would have thought that scores of movie theatres would close because movies became available on demand from Netflix, Amazon Prime, and other networks? Who would have expected Apple the computer pioneer to become a disruptive force in the telephone and music industries? And how about the popularity of K-dramas and C-dramas produced in East Asia, finding new markets in North America and Europe where streaming viewers got hooked on binge-watching them? These are only a few of the best known examples.

The key insight that we all need to be aware of is that most companies, even incumbent market leaders, are most often blindsided by innovations that come from outside their industry, from companies that aren't even on our radar screens.

In the borderless NeoWorld, you have to keep all industries and markets on your radar screen so you can see disruptive innovations coming. This is important because innovations that pop up from a different industry can make your products obsolete overnight. They can knock your company off a leadership position and destroy an entire industry.

After a century of industry dominance, Kodak's film-based photo empire was destroyed in a few years by digital photography. Compact digital camera sales fell 97% from 2009 to 2019 as a direct result of cameras embedded in smartphones. Blockbuster Video's movie rental business was wiped out by streaming media that made movies available on home cable networks. Aerial drones, which were originally developed as toys, helped Ukraine resist the Russian invasion and made the use of battlefield tanks almost obsolete.

In the NeoWorld, managers at all levels need to maintain a very large radar screen that allows them to monitor developments in other industries and markets as well as their own. They need to remain alert to new possibilities that present themselves and adopt a "borderless" mentality which means innovations can come from anywhere.

Many Neo-Innovations Come from Combining Two or More Technologies Some of the best and most valuable Neo-Innovations are developed by linking unrelated technologies from different fields of science, medicine, and commerce.

Nanotechnology—which came from physics labs—was applied to the field of molecular medicine to create *nanomedicine.* Nanotechnology began with research that gave us the ability to view and manipulate nanoscale materials and processes. Applying this innovation to medicine gave us nanomedicine, which allows us to view and manipulate biological processes and structures to create novel medical therapies at the nanoscale.

At Tesla, Elon Musk has been combining chip technology, mobile communication, and neuroscience to create a device that can be implanted in the brain to enable someone who is paralyzed to communicate, use a computer, or walk.

The combination of GPS tracking, mapping software, and voice synthesis gave us the navigation aids that keep us from getting lost when we drive to a new destination. In the NeoWorld, it was the combination of navigation and autopilot technologies that turned self-driving cars from a possibility to a reality.

Combining technologies isn't the exclusive domain of sophisticated apps. Many routine functions are being turned into something new and special simply by combining technologies. For example, several companies have created wireless motorized window blinds that can be adjusted using a remote control or voice command. Instead of twisting a plastic rod or tugging on a rope, you just say, "Close the blinds," and the blinds automatically adjust!

There are lots of ways to combine functions using technologies that are cheaper and easier to use than ever before. If you can think of something ordinary that would benefit from being automated or voice controlled, you may have the next million dollar innovation.

Mixing and matching different technologies is one of the best ways to create an entirely new innovation or solve a sticky problem. One of the best things about the NeoWorld is that we are all becoming more familiar with very complex technologies such as generative AI smart software and hardware, space technologies, the Internet of Things, and vehicle navigation systems, to name a few. Many apps we use today rely on several different technologies whose value comes from a "new harmonic" created by different technologies playing different notes on the innovation piano. A harmonic is a new sound that comes from playing two different notes together. Innovations are the harmonics—the "new sounds"—of the NeoWorld.

Anyone Can Be an Innovator You don't have to be an engineer, programmer, or marketeer to be an innovator in today's "NeoWorld." You can be self-taught or gain special knowledge or expertise that allows you to develop and implement a new technology or application.

You don't have to be a scientist, engineer, or programmer to get involved with innovation. You can help promote something new simply by posting online why you like it, how you use it, or what your friends think about it. You can be an "innovation champion" and help influence innovations that you like (or hate) by reading about new developments, becoming an early adopter, and sharing information online. Early adopters are the first to use a new product or service. They're also the first to appreciate and gain the value from Neo-Innovations.

Sometimes how you use a technology is more important than the technology itself, in which case an entrepreneur who understands the value of an innovation and applies it in a way makes more profits than the original inventor.

In the era of social media, anyone can study science and technology, identify some needs, tap into communities of interest, brainstorm ideas, and even create crowdfunded organizations and projects supported by all kinds of people who share your vision. The NeoWorld is making it easy to study, collaborate, and contribute to the innovation process. Social media networks help us connect and collaborate.

It's important to keep up to date with new developments in science and technology; however, it's even more important to understand which innovations are moving from concept to commercial use because innovation is the implementation of something new. To make something happen, we need to use an innovator's toolkit, which is a set of best practices and strategies that help us move innovations from ideas to commercial products and services.

4

Neo-Innovation: Best Practices and Strategies

In this chapter I present some of the best practices and strategies that product managers, engineers, and scientists are using to develop new ideas and solutions in the NeoWorld. Neo-Innovators are benefiting from a portfolio of new tools and techniques that are more widely available and easier to use. This is an exciting time to be involved in any aspect of innovation, whether you're a developer, decision-maker, user, or hobbyist.

Traditional Best Practices

Most of the best practices in the field of innovation are well established. These concepts were developed by business school faculty who studied the best companies and industries to identify their formulas for success. I became familiar with these (and helped develop some) during my tenure at the Wharton School where I was managing director of three innovation research initiatives.

© The Author(s), under exclusive license to Springer Nature Switzerland AG 2024
M. S. Tomczyk, *Neo-Innovation*, Business Guides on the Go,
https://doi.org/10.1007/978-3-031-74303-0_4

These best practices and sense-making frameworks are applicable to any industry or market, including those that apply to innovation in the NeoWorld:

1. **What's Needed? What's Possible?** My favorite sense-making framework for developing any innovation is based on a concept originally developed by the brilliant corporate innovator, Larry Huston, who led innovation at Procter & Gamble. This concept is called "What's Needed/What's Possible?" This is the simplest and most effective framework for developing any innovation. It is elegant, it is easy to use, and it works (Fig. 4.1).

First of all, think of something that's needed in the marketplace, such as better smarter robots. Then conduct research and brainstorm ideas to determine what's possible, either now or in the future. Conduct "fact-finding" to find connections between what's needed and what's possible. If something is needed now but doesn't exist, that's a good target for a research project.

Often something that's needed already exists in an entirely different industry, but no one knows about it. For example, companies that were making telephones in the 1990s certainly didn't expect Apple, a personal computer company, to develop the iPhone. Record companies didn't expect Apple to develop iTunes which put almost all music online and almost single-handedly made records, tapes, and CDs obsolete.

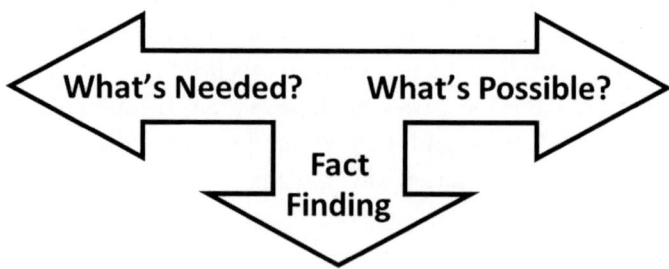

Fig. 4.1 The simplest and most elegant framework for developing an innovation asks two simple questions, what's needed and what's possible?, and relies on fact-finding and research to discover possibilities that already exist or need to be developed. (Source: M. Tomczyk)

Fact-finding is the most important part of this process. It's easy to identify something we need. It will typically be either a problem that needs to be solved or a new opportunity for a new product or service. Fact-finding reveals what's possible. That could be something that exists today, which can only be found by scouring lots of sources to see what's available now or what's being developed in labs that could be applied and commercialized. If the solution exists, a strategy might be to acquire the technology or license it.

If a possibility does not yet exist or maybe only exists in science fiction, it may need to be developed. That means creating an R&D project or working with a university, a science lab, or technology firm, to create the solution.

In the current "new era" where everything is visible and seamless, it's easier than ever to quickly search the world for pockets of innovation that might have a solution you're looking for. That makes the innovation process faster, easier, and more affordable.

2. **Create an Innovation Map.** A great way to conceptualize what's needed and what's possible is to create an *innovation map*. This is an infographic that visually maps the technologies and applications in a specific area of innovation such as robotics or nanomedicine. An innovation map can include macro- or micro-information and can be as general or detailed as you like. Sometimes it helps to create a map just to show what's happening in a particular market right now. You can also create future maps showing what's possible in the future.

To create an innovation map, select a major innovation such as artificial intelligence, self-driving vehicles, nanomedicine, or social media and then show the technologies and applications in that particular ecosystem. The examples you show can be innovations that need to be invented, developed, improved, and/or commercialized.

Innovation maps are a great example of infographics. Infographics are used to show leading competitors in an industry, to create word clouds, show interactions, illustrate various types of processes such as supply chains, and make statistics more interesting.

Here is an innovation map I created to show "robot forms and functions." This map shows types of robots that are available now as well as some that are expected to be ready in the near future (Fig. 4.2). Infographics are a great way to clearly depict and map complex relationships, time lines, processes, market sectors, competitors, and families of technologies and apps that comprise innovation ecosystems. These graphics are easily shared during video meetings, shared as email attachments, published on websites, and included in slide presentations, and information on the graphic can be linked to files and websites so viewers can drill deeper into a particular topic.

Industrial Robots
(Mechanical Arms, Automated Transport, Assembly Systems)

Robotic Vehicles
(Self Driving Vehicles, Remote Controlled Fleets, Robotic Taxis, Delivery Drones}

Smart Devices
(Internet of Things, Cloud Connected Devices, Smart Appliances, Robotic Surgeons, AI Sensors)

Wearable Robotics
(Bionic Limbs, Brain-Computer Interfaces, Exoskeletons, Power Enhancing Accessories)

Science Fiction
(Books, Articles, Movies, TV/Video, Video Games, Websites)

ROBOT
Innovation Map

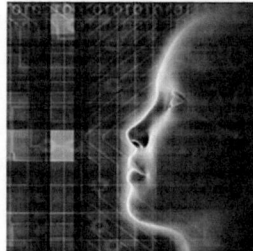

Robotic Weapons
(Airborne/Seaborne Drones, Smart Missiles; Anti-Missile Domes; Robot Armies; Unmanned Ships & Aircraft)

Humanoid Robots
(Companion Robots, Animatronics, Digital Immortality/robot Versions of Ourselves)

Androids
(Teaching, Medicine, Entertainment)

Digital Assistants
(Alexa, Siri, Google Assistant; Chatbots Generative A.I.)

Bionic Implants
(Brain-Computer Interfaces; Bionic Limbs, Artificial Organs)

Fig. 4.2 Creating an innovation map is a good way to visually describe an innovation market, industry, or ecosystem. This map depicts some of the most promising technologies and applications for robots that are already transforming the future. (Source: M. Tomczyk)

You can use a variety of applications to create infographics such as Microsoft Publishing, PowerPoint, and Photoshop. AI generators can already create graphic images including infographics, based on data and graphic guidelines you provide. DALL-E, introduced in 2021, is a good example of an AI system that can create realistic images and art from a description in natural language. DALL-E was created by OpenAI which also created ChatGPT.

3. **Ambidexterity.** Organizations that want to compete, survive, and succeed in industries that are being transformed by emerging technologies need to become *ambidextrous*. Ambidextrous means being able to do two things equally well.

In the field of innovation, ambidexterity means offering (or testing) radical new innovations while simultaneously offering traditional or "legacy" products.

It's not easy to be ambidextrous. If you manage a company, government agency, or task group, it's easy to get trapped doing things the same old way, especially if you're good at it and the old way is still generating revenues. The danger is getting trapped in the past while a new development emerges and renders the old ways obsolete.

There are numerous examples of companies that were blindsided by innovations that suddenly appeared that came from other industries. For example, music CD makers didn't expect a computer company like Apple to disrupt the music business with iTunes. Movie theatres didn't expect Netflix and other streaming services to disrupt the movie theatre industry.

Disruptive innovations can also come from changes in society in general. That's what happened when the pandemic struck. Suddenly diners couldn't eat inside restaurants. Movie theatres were closed. People started banking online to avoid standing in teller lines. Shoppers bought merchandise online, and many shopping centers had to shrink or close altogether.

During the pandemic, dozens of retail chains were forced to close store locations, restructure their operations, file for bankruptcy, or go out of business altogether. Retailers affected in the United States included Lord & Taylor, Neiman Marcus, Brooks Brothers, and Bed Bath & Beyond.

The disruptive innovators included Amazon and Alibaba which were perfectly positioned to sell and deliver products to customers during the lockdowns and quarantines.

The companies that did well during these changes were those that became ambidextrous. Restaurants offered home delivery and curbside service. Moviemakers began licensing their films to streaming networks as well as movie chains. Retailers offered in-store pickup as well as home delivery. These are examples of ambidexterity—embracing new ways of doing business while maintaining existing approaches.

I would suggest that organizations that want to compete in the NeoWorld can't just become ambidextrous. They need to become *multidextrous*. This means being involved in many emerging technologies simultaneously. In many industries, several innovations are emerging, and we still don't know which ones will become dominant, so it makes sense to have a foothold in several innovations, to make sure you're ready when one or more catch fire.

A good example of multidexterity is the climate change industry. When global warming and melting glaciers became real concerns, companies and interest groups asked "what's needed" to stabilize the climate. The big question is how do we replace gas-powered vehicles and coal-fired factories that generate greenhouse gases that cause climate change?

In the United States and Europe, the power industry is developing a combination of "clean coal" plants, hydroelectric plants, wind and solar farms, and nuclear power. The global power industry is forced to remain multidextrous until alternative energy solutions become more efficient and economical or until one alternative power source becomes dominant.

The auto industry is a good example of a multidextrous industry. Most vehicle manufacturers offer gas and diesel-powered cars and trucks but also offer fully electric vehicles as well as hybrids that combine electric and gas; hydrogen and solar powered vehicles are also being tested.

A new generation of self-driving vehicles (SDVs) is also being developed that include various types of driver-assist functions. Self-driving vehicles can be semi-autonomous or fully autonomous. Some don't even have steering wheels.

In practical use, self-driving vehicles that are fully autonomous make sense if the vehicle is a bus or shuttle that travels the same route over and over, back and forth, or if it only has to navigate a limited known map such as a shopping mall or university campus. Driverless vehicles called "robotaxis" are being road tested by Google's Waymo project, by Uber, and by other on-demand taxi services. SDVs are also being tested in China and other East Asian countries, on bus and shuttle routes.

One of the big selling features of autonomous vehicles is the safety factor, since SDVs can be programmed to maintain safe driving distances, follow traffic safety rules, and, in theory, respond faster to dangerous situations.

The innovators who are developing self-driving vehicles are integrating a wide range of technologies that include sensors, optical scanners, LIDAR, wireless navigation systems, and security which together form an SDV ecosystem. Here is an innovation map I created that describes a self-driving vehicle "ecosystem" (Fig. 4.3).

4. **Scenario Planning.** For several years, I was privileged to work with Paul J.H. Schoemaker in the Mack Center for Technological Innovation, at The Wharton School. In 2006 I coauthored (with Paul Schoemaker) a seminal research report entitled, "The Future of BioSciences: Four Scenarios for 2020 and Their Implications for Human Healthcare."[1]

Paul pioneered the concept of scenario planning which is a method of visualizing the future by painting scenarios of the future.[2] The technique involves analyzing and comparing several different possible futures and developing strategies to compete and prevail, regardless of which scenario becomes dominant. Sometimes we don't really know which path the future will take. Scenario planning allows us to visualize and prepare for several different paths.

The process of painting and preparing for several different futures often reveals hidden opportunities (and pitfalls) that decision-makers at all levels need to be aware of. In an era where uncertainty dominates

---

[1] Paul J.H. Schoemaker and Michael Tomczyk; The Future of Biosciences: Four Scenarios for 2020 and Their Implications for Human Healthcare; Mack Center/Wharton; January 2007.
[2] Paul J.H. Schoemaker, Scenario Planning: A Tool for Strategic Thinking; Sloan Management Review; November 1995.

Manufacturing

(Build, Modify, Retrofit)

Control Systems

(Autopilot, Remote, Driver Override, Voice Controls)

Sensing Systems

(Optical, LIDAR, Laser, Sonar)

Human-Vehicle Interfaces

(Controls, Over-rides, Seating, Apps)

Self Driving Vehicle ECOSYSTEM

Communications

(Cloud Links, 5G, On Demand, Ride-calling Apps, Voicecom)

Navigation Systems

(GPS, LIDAR, Localized Maps, Boundaries)

Obstacle Avoidance

(Image Databases, Recognition & Response)

Situational Awareness

(Situation Responses, Image & Video ID, Learning/Sharing)

Legal/Government

(Laws, Standards, State & Local Rules, Insurance)

Fig. 4.3 This innovation map depicts the many factors that are needed to engineer a self-driving vehicle (SDV). Together, these constitute an innovation ecosystem. (Source: M. Tomczyk)

every aspect of our lives, we need to prepare ourselves to face whatever might happen. It helps to think about all the things that might affect our lives, our families, our companies, and our jobs. The old saying—chance favors the prepared mind—is really true.

5. **The Fortune at the Bottom of the Pyramid.** During my tenure at the Wharton School, I was honored to participate in planning workshops hosted by the late C.K. Prahalad. C.K. developed the concept that large populations in poorer countries can be profitable for companies that know how to adapt to large underserved markets. He called his concept "The Fortune at the Bottom of the Pyramid."[3]

---

[3] C.K. Prahalad; The Fortune At the Bottom of the Pyramid; Wharton School Publishing; August 2004.

C.K. suggested that instead of selling 2-L bottles of soda to customers in India, Coca-Cola should consider selling small bottles that cost 5 cents each. True, the profit per bottle might be lower, but the company could sell as many as a billion 5 cent bottles per day! Doing that requires a different mindset, and this is especially true when taking a product developed for the United States or European market and moving it into a market in South America or South Asia.

Today, in the NeoWorld, an exciting Neo-Innovation that I personally am involved in developing is a neobanking SuperApp that allows unbanked customers to use their mobile phones to access banking services. Unbanked customers are people who live in rural or remote areas without access to a physical bank branch.

In some developing countries, as many as 40% of the population do not live near a bank, but in those countries almost 100% of the people have access to mobile phones. In this example, *what's needed* is a way for unbanked people in South Asia, Latin America, or other regions, to access modern banking services. *What's possible* is providing neobanking applications that allow them to do their banking using their smartphones.

6. **Deep Dialog.** Innovation cultures combine the three Cs—connectivity, communication, and collaboration. In the NeoWorld, it's often said that there are no rules. This means that anyone can connect and collaborate with anyone else.

Wharton Professor Howard Perlmutter, who I knew and admired greatly, developed a concept called Deep Dialog which stresses the importance of face-to-face meetings that offer opportunities to bond, band together, and build trust. In the NeoWorld where online meetings are replacing office meetings, it's important to keep in mind that face-to-face meetings are still relevant and helpful. One way to do this is to supplement online video chats with periodic workshops that bring together teams to discuss in person the critical issues, plans, projects, and needs and possibilities.

Neo-Innovator Tips, Tricks, and Tools

This is a rich, vibrant, exciting time to be an innovator. If you're involved—or want to be involved—in developing Neo-Innovations, there are some tips, tricks, and tools you need to be aware of. Here are some practical ideas you can use to develop radical innovations.

Open Innovation   A great way to get involved in Neo-Innovation is to join an open innovation community. Open innovation is a great way to generate better and cheaper solutions that can help reduce pollution in the environment, eliminate harmful additives from a food product, or provide air and water to a human colony on Mars or the Moon.

The term "open innovation" was coined in 2003 by UC-Berkeley Professor Henry Chesbrough, who suggested that the innovation process should be opened to everyone associated with the organization.[4] He was one of the first thought leaders to describe the "new era" of innovation where everyone can be involved in the innovation process.[5]

Companies that promote open innovation invite everyone to submit ideas and solutions, including employees, customers, dealers, partners, students, and hobbyists. Cash awards and prizes may be offered to reward those whose ideas are adopted. Some of the first organizations to adopt open innovation include 3M, Procter & Gamble, GE, and NASA.

An early pioneer was InnoCentive.com, a crowdsourcing venture that invited companies to post specific requests for radical innovations and breakthrough solutions, along with cash awards to the winner(s). Client companies were dubbed "solution seekers," and innovators who submitted ideas were called "problem-solvers." In two decades, InnoCentive developed a network of 500,000 problem-solvers, ran over 2500 challenges, and awarded over $60 million. In 2020 InnoCentive was acquired by Wazoku and became WazokuCrowd.

---

[4] Henry Chesbrough; Open Innovation: The New Imperative for Creating and Profiting from Technology; HBS Press; 2003.
[5] Henry Chesbrough; New Frontiers in Open Innovation; Oxford; 2014.

Borderless Markets If you're in any area of sales, you need to think in terms of borderless markets. Being able to connect and communicate with anyone in the world has made geographic locations, time zones, and cultural barriers irrelevant, opening exciting new opportunities for Neo-Innovators. Because there are no boundaries in the NeoWorld, companies are no longer defined by geographic borders or markets. A new generation of digital platforms allows the use of smartphones and laptops to seamlessly conduct business across international borders.

Fintech ventures and money services providers (MSBs) are an excellent example of borderless marketing. These nonbank financial service providers offer a variety of services including cross-border money transfers, bill payments, international business transactions, money storage, currency conversion, and other services that previously were the exclusive domain of banks and firms like Western Union. Fintechs and MSBs use emerging technologies such as blockchain recordkeeping and mobile banking apps to lower transaction costs and speed processing.

Borderless marketing has also transformed international retail sales. In the NeoWorld, today it's as easy to order a shirt directly from a supplier in China as it is to order a shirt from Macys. Many cross-border products are marketed on social media using personalized pop-up ads that promote direct sales from various countries. In 2023 e-commerce (online) sales exceeded $6 trillion worldwide.

SuperApps It's no longer sufficient to develop a stand-alone, single-use application. Today, most innovations in the software sector incorporate multiple functions, and every year we're seeing more SuperApps. A SuperApp provides multiple services in one application and is typically accessed via smartphone or laptop.

One of the SuperApps we're all familiar with is Microsoft Office—a portfolio of applications that includes a word processor (Word), spreadsheet (Excel), slideshow creator (PowerPoint), email and calendar app (Outlook), and other functions. Microsoft Office was originally introduced by Bill Gates in 1988.

In the NeoWorld, SuperApp platforms are being developed that provide access to several functions on a smartphone. Fintech Ecosystem Development Corporation (which I helped launch in 2021 as a founding board member) is developing a SuperApp that allows the use of a smartphone to transfer funds across borders, manage investments, store money, pay bills, apply for loans, and conduct a variety of mobile banking transactions.

Blockchain The NeoWorld is replacing paper recordkeeping and processing with digital/distributed recordkeeping. In the Fintech and MSB market, paper recordkeeping is rapidly being replaced by blockchain which is a distributed ledger system that records and saves transactions on all the computers in a shared network.

Blockchain got its start as a way to record cryptocurrency transactions. Today, blockchains are being used to digitally document transactions in many non-crypto industries and applications, and these non-crypto applications are providing new applications for blockchain developers. High-level technical innovations are making blockchains more secure, reliable, robust, and scalable.

ChatGPT Is Our New Innovation Partner One of the most visible and fastest-growing Neo-Innovations is generative AI, a type of artificial intelligence that uses natural language interfaces to create new content such as text, search results, publications, images, videos, and audio. GenAI is being used to predict maintenance needs, improve customer interactions, manage supply chains, analyze complex proteins, and develop new drug molecules.

One of the first and most popular AI algorithms is a chatbot called ChatGPT which was developed by OpenAI in collaboration with Microsoft and introduced in November 2022. ChatGPT can be used to help create many types of content including ideas for Neo-Innovations.

While I was writing this book, I was looking for some new ideas for product names for a SuperApp we're working on in a company I cofounded. I popped on ChatGPT and typed, "Please suggest some science-based product names for our application." I received a dozen suggestions that helped us choose our final brand names. This made our creative process faster and more efficient. Since then, I routinely use

ChatGPT to ask questions and get better faster replies than I would normally get from a search engine.

The Internet of Things If you want to create a new device of some sort, you should think about something that connects to the Internet. One of the major trends in the past decade involves connecting physical devices to the Internet and online systems, which is called the Internet of Things (IoT).

In the past, when we developed a new product, we thought in terms of a device such as a smartphone or drone or a software application. Today, a host of digital wireless innovations are helping to create smart devices, smart homes, and smart cities.

In virtually every city in the world, CCTV cameras monitor streets, homes, shopping malls, and stores. Video systems monitor climate, weather patterns, and traffic patterns and provide security for people in stores and on the street. Millions of people have video doorbells connected to the Internet that alert us when we receive a package or if there is an intruder lurking at the door.

By 2024 there will be as many as 15 billion devices connected to the Internet of Things (IoT), doubling to 30 billion by 2030.

Miniaturize, Automate, and Accelerate Making something that is smaller, faster, and automated is still a proven formula for developing a winning innovation. During the pandemic, people who had to stay home more did more cooking so there was a need for faster, more efficient countertop cooking appliances.

What's needed was a cooking device that could make foods fast like a microwave but also make them crispy. One of the innovations that addressed that need was the air fryer, a countertop version of a convection oven, which circulates hot air to make foods crispy with little or no oil and can also reheat and thaw foods. Air fryers "caught fire" (pun intended) during the pandemic. By the end of 2020, a third of all US homes owned an air fryer, which increased to 60% in 2023. So many people adopted air fryers that a new need was created. Frozen food makers responded by offering "air fryer-ready" vegetables and meats.

Include Young People on Innovation Teams It is essential to include young people on development teams. There are two reasons for this: (1) young men and women do not know what can't be done so they have no limits or boundaries, and (2) they're closer to emerging technologies and understand the potential better than older people.

Here's a story from my own experience: A few years ago, I was invited by a government intelligence agency to participate in a small workshop designed to help identify emerging technologies that the intel community should be aware of and prepare for. We brainstormed for a couple of days, using groupware and computers to capture our ideas, and came up with a list of technologies the intel community should monitor.

At the end of the last session, the workshop leader looked around and said, "Does anyone have any questions?" to which I replied, "Yes. How many of you in this room are under the age of thirty? Raise your hand." *Nobody raised their hands.* So then I asked, "What's wrong with this picture?"

Everyone laughed, but soon after that, the workshop leader contacted me and said, "Michael, we took your advice. The day after the workshop we rounded up every intern and admin in the office and put them through the same exercise, and we got eight ideas no one thought of before!"

Here's another great idea for brainstorming sessions: make sure to provide input methods for introverts. In my experience, introverts are some of the smartest people because they internalize their thinking although they don't always express their ideas in open meetings. One way to address this is to give everyone in a brainstorming meeting access to "groupware" that lets everyone type in their ideas and inputs. If a meeting is dominated by "extroverts" who sometimes hog the spotlight and do most of the talking, groupware allows introverts to quietly share their ideas, and often their ideas, delivered quietly, are some of the best ideas.

Thought Leaders We Need to Learn From If you'd like to learn more about innovation in general, or drill down deeper on a particular topic, you can gain a lot of insights by reading articles, books, and speeches by academic and industry thought leaders whose original thinking has given us the sensemaking frameworks used today by innovation professionals.

Management research faculty at Wharton, Harvard, Columbia, and other leading business schools worked closely with industry and government leaders to identify and develop "better practices" to enhance the innovator's toolkit. Their publications are a great source of inspiration for anyone involved in developing or applying Neo-Innovations.

5

You Can Learn from Innovation Gurus

If you want to know what's coming next, it's a good idea to monitor what innovation gurus are working on, especially serial innovators. If you look at the biographies of the world's best innovators, you can see from their diverse backgrounds that there is a special group of people in the world that seem to have innovation in their DNA.

To show that I practice what I preach, I used ChatGPT to generate a core list of technology leaders. Using ChatGPT is really easy. To generate a list of "gurus," I asked ChatGPT, "Who are the most influential technology leaders today?" A list of world-class innovators with job titles and achievements was generated in less than a minute. I added some names along with some notes and quotes and listed them here in alphabetical order.

This group of 16 innovation leaders is a good group of "Neo-Innovators" to study and monitor, because their achievements are classic examples of radical innovation. They are all still active, we can expect more achievements during their careers, and their future innovations have a high probability of success:

© The Author(s), under exclusive license to Springer Nature Switzerland AG 2024
M. S. Tomczyk, *Neo-Innovation*, Business Guides on the Go,
https://doi.org/10.1007/978-3-031-74303-0_5

1. **Anthony Atala**—Founding director of the Wake Forest Institute for Regenerative Medicine, where he leads a team of more than 400 medical researchers. Dr. Atala is a bioengineer, urologist, and pediatric surgeon. He is a pioneer in the development of innovative therapies for replacing and repairing diseased or damaged organs and tissue. Dr. Atala and his team developed the first lab-grown organ (a human bladder) which was successfully implanted into a patient. He created the first 3D bioprinters used to "print" tissues and organs. He holds more than 250 patents. His work has been listed twice in *Time Magazine*'s top 10 medical breakthroughs of the year.

2. **Jeff Bezos**—Founder of Amazon. Amazon's amazing teams continue to "Neo-Innovate" in AI, e-commerce, warehouse automation/robotics, cloud computing, streaming media (Amazon Prime), aerial drone delivery (Prime Air), digital publishing (Kindle), robotics (Amazon Astro), smart doorbells (Ring), and their iconic digital voice assistant (Alexa). According to Amazon, Alexa is connected to more than 300 million devices and is a major enabling technology in smart homes. Amazon's Alexa Fund invests in technologies and start-ups that are advancing the development of ambient computing, new media, and the future of smart devices.

3. **Greg Brockman**—Cofounder and president of OpenAI, which developed ChatGPT and GPT-4, the first commercially available generative artificial intelligence application. Brockman believes new developments in artificial intelligence are changing the world. He has said, "We're clearly moving to a world where (the Internet) is alive. You can talk to it, and it understands you and helps you."[1]

4. **Tim Cook**—CEO of Apple, the personal computer pioneer founded by Steve Jobs and Steve Wozniak. Apple continues to introduce Neo-Innovations including the AppleWatch, HomePod, smarter iPhones and iPads, and new features for the Apple Music (iTunes) app. Apple also worked on the development of an electric vehicle (Apple iCar).

5. **Dr. Jennifer Doudna**—Professor of molecular and cell biology and chemistry at UC-Berkeley and founder of Mammoth Biosciences.

---

[1] Carlson, Kara; OpenAI founder talks ChatGPT, Dall-E and what's next for artificial intelligence at SXS@; Austin American-Statesman; 11 March 2023.

Dr. Doudna was awarded the 2020 Nobel Prize in Chemistry (shared with collaborator Dr. Emmanuelle Charpentier) for work on the CRISPR gene editing system, which reduced the time and effort needed to precisely edit genomic DNA. CRISPR allows researchers to easily edit DNA sequences and modify genes. Applications include treating genetic and protein disorders (such as sickle cell anemia) and engineering improved types of crops. CRISPR is not only used in medical research labs and clinical trials but is also easy enough to use that it is used to teach genetic engineering in high school classrooms. One thing to watch for in the coming months and years is the commercialization of CRISPR and other gene editing tools, making it possible to edit disease-causing genes like we edit bits and bytes in software programs.

6. **Anita Goel, MD., Ph.D.**—Chair and CEO of Nanobiosym Diagnostics, where she oversees product design, engineering, clinical trials, regulatory approvals, and manufacturing of breakthrough technologies including Gene-RADAR and related apps for providing personalized precision medicine including mobile precision testing for COVID. She is a leading physicist, physician, and scientist in the emerging field of nanobiophysics and is a pioneer in the field of nanomedicine. Dr. Goel has over 80 patents worldwide. She served on the Committee on Manufacturing Innovation of the National Academy of Engineering and Canadian Institute for Advanced Research and on the Nanotechnology and Scientific Advisory Boards of Lockheed Martin and PepsiCo. In 2020 Barclay's Bank selected Nanobiosym as one of the world's top 10 companies solving the global COVID crisis.

In addition to Dr. Goel, I would like to recognize several scientists and entrepreneurs whose research and innovative achievements contributed to the rapid creation of vaccines which effectively stopped the spread of COVID. These include Dr. Katalin Kariko and Dr. Drew Weissman who developed the mRNA vaccine technology that contributed to the success of COVID-19 vaccines from Pfizer, Moderna, and others. Dr. Ozlem Tureci contributed to the BioNTech-Pfizer vaccine and Dr. Albert Bouria, the CEO at Pfizer.

7. **David Hanson, Ph.D.**—CEO and founder of Hanson Robotics. Dr. Hanson is a pioneer in the design of humanoid robots, including Sophia the first robot to be granted citizenship (by Saudi Arabia in 2017). He believes that humanoid features and attributes make robots more acceptable in many applications such as serving as a tutor, teacher, companion, receptionist, or security guard.

8. **Reed Hastings**—Cofounder and executive chairman of Netflix, which led the way in streaming media and original content production. Netflix created a unique corporate innovation culture called "freedom and responsibility" which allows employees to manage their time.

    During the pandemic, Netflix and other streaming media transformed how we access and watch movies and TV and "disintermediated" movie theatre attendance and network TV viewing, by offering top quality content on demand. When theatres were closed for 6 months to a year, millions of people increased their use of Netflix and other streaming media, which redefined home entertainment in the NeoWorld. Hasting's 2020 book, *No Rules: Netflix and the Culture of Reinvention*, describes the company's innovation culture and was a *New York Times* bestseller.

9. **Jensen Huang**—Cofounder and CEO of NVIDIA, a trillion-dollar corporation and world leader in artificial intelligence hardware and software, including graphic processing units (GPUs), AI chips, and other innovations. NVIDIA chips are used to power a wide range of innovations including the next generation of computers, generative AI systems, drug discovery systems, and autonomous vehicles. NVIDIA's Clara™ system is a GPU-accelerated computational drug discovery platform that combines AI, data analytics, simulation, and visualization. In September 2023 Jensen Huang told Columbia Business School students interested in becoming innovators: "You should choose something that somehow you're destined to do—either a set of qualities about your personality or your expertise, or the people you're surrounded by, your scale, whatever your perspective, whatever you're somehow destined to do. (And) you better love

working on that thing so much because, unless you do, the pain and suffering is going to be too great."[2]

10. **Ray Kurzweil**—Computer scientist, author, inventor, and futurist. Kurzweil has asserted that in the future, everyone will live forever. He has also predicted the convergence of humans and machines. In 2013, Kurzweil predicted that in 15 years, medical technology could add more than a year to one's remaining life expectancy for each year that passes, and we could then "outrun our own deaths." He also predicted that by the late 2020s, it will be impossible to distinguish reality from virtual reality, and as we can see from what's happening online, this is already happening.

11. **Jack Ma**—Cofounder and executive chairman of Alibaba Group based in Hangzhou, China. Alibaba is the world's largest online commerce company. Alibaba is adopting Neo-Management principles by converting the company from a centralized enterprise to a decentralized holding company comprised of a group of seven business units including Cainiao, an intelligent logistics network; online shopping sites Taobao and Tmall; and Alibaba Cloud Computing, a local services group, international commerce, and entertainment. Jack Ma has stated that his goal is to help more people make "sustainable money" that is "not only good for themselves but also good for society."

12. **Kiran Mazumdar-Shaw**—Executive chair and founder of Biocon Ltd. and Biocon Biologics Ltd., biotechnology leaders based in Bangalore, India, and former chair of the Indian Institute of Management. She is an award winning entrepreneur and world-class biosciences pioneer. She started Biocon in 1978 in the garage of her rented house, selling an enzyme extracted from papaya. Within a year she was manufacturing and exporting enzymes to the United States and Europe and expanded into biopharmaceuticals. Ms. Mazumdar Shaw is a sterling example of an innovator/entrepreneur who has combined social responsibility with medical research and innovation. Biocon focuses on making drugs affordable to people in

---

[2] Wyn Jones, Roland; NVIDIA CEO Jensen Huang Reveals Keys to AI and Leadership; Columbia Business School; 4 October 2023.

developing economies, including statins and drugs used to treat cancer, diabetes, and other diseases. Biocon has filed more than 950 patents based on its research.

13. **Elon Musk**—Founder of Tesla (electric cars and energy), SpaceX (aerospace rockets, Starlink satellite network), Neuralink (brain-machine interface), and The Boring Company ("neo tunnels"). In 2021 Musk gave himself the title, TeknoKing of Tesla which is a "neo-job title"—the first time a CEO crowned himself a corporate "king." In 2022 he bought Twitter for $44 billion, and in 2023 he renamed the social platform "X."

In 2015, in a podcast interview with Neil deGrasse Tyson, Elon Musk described five things he thought would most affect the future of humanity: the Internet, sustainable energy, space exploration, artificial intelligence, and rewriting human genetics. He is clearly working to innovate in all of these domains.

The Starlink satellite constellation, which is being deployed by SpaceX, is a low-orbit fast-access communication network that deployed more than 5000 satellites since 2019, with a potential to put a total of 40,000 satellites into orbit. The Starlink constellation has the potential to make Internet access faster for everyone, including faster access to the cloud and specialized databases needed to enhance AI chatbots, smart devices and sensors, autonomous vehicles, maritime communications, climate monitoring, and military systems.

Elon Musk has also announced his intention to develop an AI chatbot called TruthGPT which he describes as "a maximum truth-seeking AI that tries to understand the nature of the universe." In 2024 Musk announced Tesla's plan to provide a "low-cost" Tesla electric vehicle, along with a robotaxi service/application using Tesla vehicles.

14. **Satya Nadella**—CEO of Microsoft, is leading Microsoft's transformation into a major player in cloud computing and artificial intelligence, as well as enterprise software, search engines, video games (Xbox), and video collaboration (Microsoft Teams). In 2014, Microsoft reassigned half its staff to a group called MSR NeXT

which is tasked to develop high-impact innovations. In 2016 the company acquired the LinkedIn business network.

15. **Sundar Pichai**—CEO of Alphabet Inc., Google's parent company, which truly changed the world with radical innovations that include Google Search, Gmail, Google Map, as well as Google Translate, Scholar, and other extensions and apps. The company's Neo-Innovations include Waymo self-driving vehicles, Google Assistant, and video meeting apps (Google Meet).

16. **Mark Zuckerberg**—Cofounder and CEO of Facebook (now Meta Platforms, Inc.), pioneered a variety of social media apps (Facebook, Instagram, WhatsApp, and Oculus) that were well situated to keep people connected during the pandemic and now are core technologies in the NeoWorld. Zuckerberg almost single-handedly created the social media revolution that keeps us all connected today.

The Role of Women in Neo-Innovation

Several of the gurus listed in this chapter are women. Many of the changes that characterize the NeoWorld are providing new gateways for women in science, technology, and business. Today it's easier than ever for women to get involved in the innovation process, thanks to AI-based search engines, social and business networks, free online libraries, and real-time science news.

Social media is helping to break down barriers and restrictions in many countries that previously posed obstacles and cultural or religious restrictions on women. Legal precedents require equal pay for comparable jobs held by men and women and restrict or minimize discrimination based on age, political or religious beliefs, and gender.

This is a good time for women to get involved in science, technology, and business. In March 2024, women inventors held only 10.9% of all US patents, including 16% of design patents and 5% of mechanical engineering patents. This suggests there is ample room for growth and participation by women innovators.

In the new era, women are adapting the practices and strategies described in this book, especially in social media where women are especially successful as online influencers, podcast speakers, and content editors. Women are also becoming more active in nanomedicine and other emerging technologies. Many extraordinary women have won prizes in initiatives designed to incentivize and recognize women innovators worldwide.

Global Initiatives for Women Innovators The US government, European Union, and United Nations have recognized the need to support women scientists and entrepreneurs. Involving more women in the innovation process will greatly increase the global pool of scientists, engineers, business leaders, and problem-solvers who are needed to grow the global economy.

Important initiatives have been established in the Mideast, South Asia, and other regions, to identify and fund women innovators and entrepreneurs. A notable example is the Women Innovators Programme established in 2021 by the United Nations Development Programme (UNDP). As part of this initiative, the UNDP's Amman Regional Hub for Arab States has supported more than 80 women innovators from 16 countries with funding, networking opportunities, and hundreds of hours of mentoring.

More opportunities are needed to provide innovation gateways and resources in remote and rural regions of the world and in developing countries. This is important because the problems of sub-Saharan Africa, Bangladesh, and the Amazon rainforest are different from problems of industrialized nations in North America and Europe.

Innovators in advanced nations tend to focus on complex "system innovations" involving software, chips, electronic devices, nanotechnology, gene editing, etc. Innovators in countries like Bangladesh or Indonesia may have different priorities such as enabling people in remote villages who don't have access to a physical bank branch to use their smartphones to do online banking, finding better solutions to reclaim deserts in sub-Saharan Africa, developing creative ways to increase crop yields, and restoring ocean reefs.

Historically, there are many notable examples of female innovators from Africa, East, and South Asia, who are working tirelessly to solve problems such as malaria and other diseases that are unique to rural, remote, and developing regions of the world.

A good example is Professor Tu Youyou, a Chinese pharmaceutical chemist who discovered a new life-saving malaria treatment called artemisinin, which quickly reduces plasmodium parasites in the blood of malaria patients. Ironically, her discovery is based on a traditional Chinese treatment that has been used since 400 A.D. Youyou and two colleagues shared the 2015 Nobel Prize in Physiology or Medicine. She became the first Chinese Nobel prize winner in this category. Professor Youyou is chief scientist at the China Academy of Chinese Medical Sciences.

Another example is Kiara Nirghin, a South African student who was only 19 years old when she won the 2016 Google Science Fair for creating a low-cost, biodegradable, superabsorbent polymer that can retain over 100 times its mass, which is useful in water conservation for sustaining crops through droughts. Her innovation is made of orange peels and avocado skins.

Segenet Kelemu, a molecular plant pathologist from Ethiopia, has developed innovations in small farm agriculture to help farmers in Africa increase their crop yields. In 2014 she was named one of the 100 most influential African women by Forbes Africa and received the L'Oreal-UNESCO Award for Women in Science.

Professor Rana Sanyal, chief scientific officer and cofounder of RS Research, is pioneering the development of smart nanomedicines used in targeted chemotherapy. She won the 2023–2024 European Prize for Women Innovators, which is awarded to recognize the development of disruptive innovations that are driving positive change in the world. Prof. Sanyal is listed as inventor or coinventor on more than 50 issued patents.

Natalia Tomiyama, managing director and cofounder of Nuwiel, won second prize in the 2024 EU competition, for her development of smart electronic trailers that can carry hundreds of pounds and uses sensors to match the movement of the person or biker pulling it. Maria Gonzalez Manso, CEO and cofounder of Marsi Bionics in Spain, won the "Rising Innovator" award in the EU competition, for her development of pediatric exoskeletons and robotic knees.

Ajaita Shah, founder of Frontier Markets, was named Social Innovator of the Year for 2024, for her contributions to providing improved access to technology and market connectivity in rural India.

In the NeoWorld there are many areas that will benefit greatly from increased participation by both men and women innovators from all parts of the world. Hopefully this book will help call attention to this need and help promote more activities to involve more participation, everywhere, in Neo-Innovation.

Part III

Neo-Management

In April 1980 I was hired as assistant to the president and marketing strategist by Jack Tramiel, founder of Commodore, the personal computer company. I was 31 years old. On my first day with the company, I attended a senior management meeting in London where Jack announced he wanted to develop a low-cost color computer. When we got back to California, I typed a detailed memo with my ideas for the new computer. On the cover I drew a caricature of myself which was a happy face with a beard and mustache.

I took the memo to Jack's office and tossed it on his desk. "What's this?" he asked.

"That's everything that needs to be done with the new computer," I said. "Make sure whoever's in charge does all these things." My memo suggested a price under $300, full-size typewriter style keys, IEEE and RS232 interfaces, and much more.

A few days later, Jack came into my office and tossed the memo on my desk. "What's this?" I asked.

"That's everything that needs to be done with the new computer," he said. "You're in charge of making it happen. I told everyone involved that anything done with this has to be approved by you. This won't be easy. You'll have to use a lot of persuasion."

"I can do that," I replied.

And that's how I became the product manager for the Commodore VIC-20, the first full-featured home computer and the first computer to sell one million units.

6

What's New About Neo-Management?

If you're a manager—managing a task, project, campaign, company, partnership, or global enterprise—you need to think more holistically about all the points of contact and connections involved. Managing a company today—which we might call Neo-Management—means managing not just the employees and tasks but also anything and anyone in the external environment who may interact in any way with the company.

The best way to visualize this is to consider that anything that can be managed can be thought of as an ecosystem (or mini-ecosystem). Managing in the new era is a form of ecosystem management.

A jungle is an ecosystem. A desert is an ecosystem. The ocean is an ecosystem and so is a small pond and even a goldfish bowl. An ecosystem encompasses everything. Some ecosystems are comprised of several mini-ecosystems which are self-contained entities that need to be managed separately but also integrated. A mini-ecosystem may include a specific market or industry, a country or region, a culture and language, or an interest group such as a bitcoin community, user group, or social network.

How we manage these ecosystems and mini-ecosystems depends on how we structure the organization. Neo-organizations can be centralized or decentralized. Decision-making can be concentrated in the C-suite or

© The Author(s), under exclusive license to Springer Nature Switzerland AG 2024
M. S. Tomczyk, *Neo-Innovation*, Business Guides on the Go,
https://doi.org/10.1007/978-3-031-74303-0_6

spread across the entire organization. In the new era we are seeing more "distributed organizations" which means an organization that can exist anywhere. Distributed organizations may or may not have a central office. The value of distributed organizations is being able to tap and engage workers, partners, and service providers wherever they exist, which may be anywhere on the planet.

These changes in the nature and structure of organizations have transformed how companies do business and have also redefined the very nature of work.

Neo-Work Is Different

It's truly amazing how much we've been forced to change and adapt by the COVID pandemic. When the pandemic shut down companies and industries, it changed the nature of work itself. This includes how and where we work, who we work with, and how we manage all this. What used to be a very clear work-life boundary was suddenly a blurry line. Millions of people were suddenly working at home.

After the pandemic when people started returning to offices and factories, they started expecting and demanding that work environments be more lifestyle friendly because they realized from working at home that you can be efficient and productive in your job and also comfortable and casual, too. You don't have to chain yourself to an office desk to build a company, even a global company. You can balance work, home life, exercise, and hobbies, and for most people the result was *more* productivity, not less. Work today—which is now Neo-Work—is not static or defined by rules and policies. Neo-Work is something we can customize and adapt to be more productive on the job while maintaining a lifestyle we choose.

Since 2020, new realities and expectations have required organizations to adopt different management approaches. Many of the new management practices that are required to succeed in the post-pandemic world are so novel that they can legitimately be called *Neo-Management.*

The new generation of workers—who we can call Neo-Workers—are not forced to work 9 to 5 in offices, factories, warehouses, and assembly lines. They are not chained to a workplace. Their workspace can be anywhere they happen to be. They can go home early or take a day off and still be at work because their smartphone and laptop are their offices.

Allowing people to work outside the office is not a "flex time" concept where workers are allowed to work at home 1 or 2 days a week. This is a concept where workers are totally mobile. The neo-workplace is not a place. That's the big change. The location is anywhere. The time is any time. If you are not in the office, at home, or maybe traveling, you can still participate because you may be disconnected physically, but you are always connected virtually.

The nice thing about Neo-Work is that you can balance your family obligations with work obligations. You can leave work early to pick up kids from school, or run some errands before stores close, or pick up groceries for dinner tonight. Those hours are not "lost time." They are part of the ebb and flow of the Neo-Workday. We are accommodating people's life schedules by making their work schedules more flexible.

The concept of Neo-Work means modern businesses can operate more like business families. The best employers recognize the need to balance work, family life, and entertainment. An office complex doesn't have to be sterile or cold. It can be warm and inviting like a university campus. Companies can have fitness centers, areas set aside for employees to relax and collect their thoughts or meet informally to brainstorm. In a Neo-Work zone, even the cafeteria food can be fun. I know of one company where lunch is free every day, but there are no tables in the cafeteria, only in the office area. So employees get free food, but they are encouraged to sit together while eating, at tables in the office area where they cultivate better work relationships, share information, and create new ideas.

Some people can work at home part of the time or all of the time. They can stay connected and complete their assignments wherever they are, which also means that they might talk on their smartphones about projects and goals while eating or walking or riding in a car or train. Instead of introducing distractions from being away from the office, Neo-Work has made everyone more productive because now work can happen wherever we are which means we're always theoretically in the work zone.

The Three Cs of Neo-Management

The three Cs of Neo-Management are connectivity, communication, and collaboration. The first C is connectivity. No matter where you are in the world, in your car, home office, or on a plane, you should be able to use your smartphone to *connect*. You also need to be able to *communicate* visually which includes videoconferencing, as well as viewing and sharing charts, spreadsheets, infographics, and PowerPoint slides in real time with whoever is connected online. It's also important to be able to *collaborate*, which means having fast, automated, easy-to-use tools and process to help make decisions and actions flow faster in real time.

All companies and managers need to be aware that the advent of low-orbit satellite constellations has enabled new forms of innovation based on faster communication. Satellite constellations are groups of satellites operating in a system to provide faster more reliable Internet access, wireless phone communication, faster GPS tracking, and more. Satellite constellation providers include Iridium, Globalstar, Orbcomm, Starlink, OneWeb, Project Kuiper (Amazon), Telesat, and Planet Labs.

Satellite constellations like Starlink have increased the speed of the Internet, making devices like robots and self-driving vehicles smarter and more responsive by giving them fast access to cloud databases needed to process large language applications such as AI chatbots.

In a "new era" company, we can create financial spreadsheets in real time during an online meeting. We can do the same with PowerPoint slides including pitch decks for investors and conference presentations. We can create and edit important documents in one session, saving time and effort.

In companies I'm involved with, we're practicing Neo-Management in many ways. For example, we describe our organizations as ecosystems. We seek to acquire and grow companies in other companies and markets. When we evaluate potential acquisitions, we specifically look for companies in countries and regions that can be considered "mini-ecosystems." Ideally, we look for acquisitions that may have a strong market position but are limited because they only have one application or need extra funding to grow. We can add more apps to their portfolio which increases sales to their existing customers and attracts new customers. Of course, to keep adding applications and creating SuperApps, we need to keep innovating.

New Best Practices and Strategies

Here are some of the most interesting characteristics of "Neo-Management" that are being reinvented today that we all need to be aware of.

1. **Companies Are Treated as Ecosystems.** In the NeoWorld, a company is no longer a structured corporation with lots of rules and policies and strict lines of authority and responsibility. A modern organization is viewed as an *ecosystem* and subsidiaries that operate in specific market environments or in foreign markets are considered *mini-ecosystems.*

    This framework forces the management team to engage not just employees but also customers, dealers and distributors, vendors and service providers, investors, the media, and influencers. Policies are designed to encourage and enhance the participation of everyone in the ecosystem. Having access to more ideas, suggestions, and people with diverse backgrounds and skillsets is opening all organizations to new sources of innovation.

2. **Decision-Making Is More Democratic.** Many organizations are moving from autocratic leadership models where a CEO acts like a dictator, to open management forms. Today, many companies have shifted to consensus management and group decision-making where many teams work independently and essentially manage themselves. Another variation is collegial management, where ideas and plans are shared with a group of colleagues and implemented when everyone is in agreement.

3. **The Work Environment Is More Relaxed.** A growing number of companies have begun to treat their employees like a "business family," and this translates into a happier, joyful, positive, positive work environment. The best companies are run like college campuses,

with a fitness center, hiking trails, and other amenities. This recognizes the reality that in the NeoWorld, lifestyle is often considered as important than work. Including "lifestyle" in the definition of work has transformed companies and industries in many interesting ways.

During the pandemic, most people were forced to work from home, and workers became accustomed to working in a relaxed environment where many workplace rules and restrictions did not exist. When they returned to work after the pandemic subsided, many workers were turned off by the artificial constraints imposed by companies and factories. They began to insist that employers pay more attention to "lifestyle needs," and this forced organizations to adopt Neo-Work practices. In most organizations, dissolving home/work boundaries resulted in increased productivity and better workforce morale and changed the nature of work itself.

4. **Workers Are Empowered.** Distributed leadership involves creating flexible teams that are able to use the newest and best emerging technologies to cope with external risks and pursue new opportunities. MIT Sloan Professor Deborah Ancona defines distributed leadership as *collaborative, autonomous practices managed by a network of formal and informal leaders across an organization.*[1] Workers at all levels are empowered. Distributed management groups can work independently with a high degree of autonomy and can also collaborate by mixing and matching teams and tasks with other groups in the organization.

5. **Workers Are Rewarded with More Free Time.** In the past, if someone finished everything really fast, the company simply piled on more work, and more, and more. The faster you worked, the more work you got! Today, smart people who figure out how to do their jobs faster and better get rewarded with *more time off* to enjoy life. If you are super productive and complete your tasks quickly, you can earn more time with your family and have more fun. Time is a commodity. The best NeoBusiness enterprises are structured to reward

---

[1] Somers, Meredith; Why distributed leadership is the future of management; MIT Management; 19 April 2022.

efficient team members with more time off. That's a huge paradigm shift from how workers used to be treated.

6. **Meetings Are "Virtual."** In the NeoWorld, most meetings and workshops are virtual, which means people in different physical locations can use their mobile or Internet-connected devices to meet in the same virtual room. Anyone can participate, wherever they are in the world. Meetings that used to be held in offices and conference rooms are now held online. Even people who are traveling can tune into a meeting from their car or plane. Video meetings allow everyone to see their colleagues and collaborators in real time. PowerPoints, spreadsheets, and infographics can be created and shared during the meeting. Documents can be signed electronically.

7. **Organizations Are Multicultural.** The NeoWorld favors multicultural organizations, not just because of the benefits that come from diversity. Because we're all connected, most geographic, cultural, and market boundaries no longer exist. In a borderless world, we can tap into the best available programmers, engineers, scientists, and marketing experts wherever they are in the world. Some of the best software programmers in the world are located in places like India and Bangladesh. These resources might have been difficult to access a few years ago, but in the NeoWorld they are just a mouse click away and available 24/7 to participate in video meetings.

8. **Global Collaboration Is Easier.** Thinking across cultures and geographic borders allows Neo-Managers to form partnerships with innovators and entrepreneurs in other countries, which provides access to a vast pool of business possibilities. In the NeoWorld, a lot of innovators have had to learn how to say "What's Possible?" in other languages, for example, *¿Qué es posible?* in Spanish or 什么是可能的 (*shénmeshì kěnéng de*) in Chinese.

9. **Many Creative Services Are Available from Online Resources.** When the pandemic trapped thousands of artists, writers, and other creative people in their homes, many started offering their services online to generate income during company lockdowns. Some websites invite potential clients to provide what's needed for a company name, logo, PowerPoint design, or advertisement and what they are prepared to pay. Ten or 20 professional freelancers are then invited to

submit mockups for the client to consider. The client selects the "winner" from actual mockups or finished artwork and often gives the winner more contract work offline. This scheme makes the creative process competitive and provides lots of variations to choose from, the fee or "reward" is known in advance, and the cost is a fraction of what projects cost a decade ago. For example, a logo design that used to cost $30,000 may only cost $3000 today.

10. **Decision-Making Is Faster.** In this new world, everyone is expected to multitask, work fast, communicate fluidly, and invest time and energy to achieve the best possible results. Results count more than formality and protocol. This carries an inherent expectation that everyone will work fast. Some CEOs say that in the NeoWorld, decisions are made "at the speed of light." Instead of circulating a document to lawyers, accountants, and executives for comment and approval and waiting days or weeks for all the approvals to come in, a document such as a legal contract can be shared online, edited by the group in real time, and signed electronically via email. Processes that used to take days or weeks can now be completed in real time.

11. **Neo-Innovators Want to Improve the World.** Before the pandemic, social consciousness was an option, not even an expectation. Some companies said they wanted to improve the world but still engaged in pollution, waste, and unsafe practices. It seems that, after the pandemic showed us how fragile life can be, there was a shift in sentiment, and more companies started focusing on improving the world.

During the pandemic, innovations in telemedicine allowed high-risk people to get medical help online instead of going to hospital emergency rooms where they might contact COVID-infected patients. Scanners were developed to take the temperature of people entering buildings, to screen for COVID symptoms. Amazon and other retailers have conducted pilot projects involving the use of aerial drones to deliver emergency packages to remote areas stranded by floods or earthquakes. On American highways, electronic toll systems like E-ZPass* replaced toll booths with cashless lanes to eliminate the handling of cash by human toll collectors and drivers. These are just a few examples.

All of us can think of innovations that will make the world a better place. We can make drugs cheaper and more available. We can provide mobile phone apps that allow unbanked people in remote parts of the world to get access to financial services. We can improve security systems in high crime communities. We can engineer climate-friendly cars, trucks, and buses that are more affordable and efficient. We can develop recyclable straws, utensils, dinnerware, and other common items that contribute to pollution. We can develop medical innovations that give us longer, healthier lives.

Almost every day when we go online, we can see the world changing as new discoveries are made, new technologies are created, and new applications make our lives more exciting and fun. All of these activities need to be managed in new and different ways that are still evolving, especially as new forms of organizations keep evolving.

7

New Forms of Organizations

Business experts and industry leaders are constantly on the lookout for new forms of organizations that can make innovation easier, cheaper, faster, and more efficient. Many new forms of organizations that were spawned during and after the pandemic are called "virtual" because they mostly exist online or in the ether of social networks and communities. Most of these new forms represent entirely new business models that were enabled by technological advances in computing power, speed, efficiency, mobility, and security.

In the post-pandemic NeoWorld, consumers gained rapid access to online shopping sites, online social networks, and streaming media. They followed and subscribed to communities of interest that gave instant access to news, information, how-to videos, and more. Consumers are able to make decisions faster, like buying something from a pop-up ad or instantly messaging friends, families, and colleagues. This super-connected, high-speed world has created several new forms of organizations.

Of all the new forms of organization that are evolving today, social media networks are the most successful. More than 4.9 billion people in

© The Author(s), under exclusive license to Springer Nature Switzerland AG 2024
M. S. Tomczyk, *Neo-Innovation*, Business Guides on the Go,
https://doi.org/10.1007/978-3-031-74303-0_7

the world were using social media in 2023, with another billion expected by 2027.

Social media started out as "communities of interest" such as software user groups on the Internet. Facebook, Instagram, TikTok, and YouTube jump-started a new era in connectivity that blossomed into huge webs of bloggers, vloggers, influencers, subscribers, followers, and fans. E-commerce sites like Amazon have also evolved into hybrid forms that are part commerce site and part social network. All of these sites draw energy from interactive chats, comments, and reviews.

Many social media sites invite subscribers to pay an annual fee to view content or get discounts on products, while others allow followers to award ratings which networks and sponsors convert into cash payments or prizes. Others rely on advertisers and sponsors who compensate the sites based on active viewers and clicks to sponsored links. Thinking ahead to what the next generation of social media might look like, we can expect to see more creative ways to provide personalized content as well as better ways to reward followers and capture profits from social interactions.

Here are a few of the new forms of organizations that have transformed the social media industry in the NeoWorld:

- **Influencers and Vloggers.** In just a few short years, we've seen the rise of instant celebrities who have the ability to influence millions of fans and followers who subscribe to their webcasts. Many present daily online video blogs called "vlogs" which have themes such as travel, cooking, comedy, fashion, sports, news, or music.

    These vlogs are a new form of organization where someone creates, edits, and uploads videos on a social media platform. These vlogs generate profits from sold-out appearances by performers, sales of products associated with the influencers, sponsored ads, or earning financial "stars" from fans. Some vloggers have become millionaires from sharing their opinions online and building a loyal fanbase. The profits from this emerging industry can be enormous. Some vloggers earn $40,000 or more per month which is $480,000 per year. Compare this to the salary of most company CEOs which is $250,000 to $350,000 per year.

An influencer's impact can be favorable or unfavorable. Some of the most famous influencers include the Kardashians and many others. In 2023, Cristiano Ronaldo, the Portuguese soccer star, had more than 500 million followers. Fashion blogger Charli D'Amelio has over 200 million followers, and fashionista Chiara Ferragni has more than 27 million followers on Instagram. Jimmy Donaldson (MrBeast) has over 300 million followers. Ismo the Finnish comedian has over 280,000 subscribers. Former President Donald Trump is the most famous and successful political influencer. Taylor Swift is the most successful performer in the world by any measure, so her influence is enormous.

Most influencers are associated with sponsors and product lines, but many are simply online presenting their opinions in daily online podcasts, blogs, and vlogs. Often the media quotes influencers as experts when they may or may not be well informed or factual. What constitutes an influencer is highly subjective and is often based more on the individual's fame and popularity than knowledge or facts.

• **AI Influencers.** One of the weirdest twists on the rise of influencers is the emergence of AI influencers. Generative AI technology is being used to create conversational avatars who pose as real-life influencers. These fake influencers can be programmed to interact with online followers, comment on various issues, express opinions designed to influence followers, and promote new products and services.

CGI-generated influencers can engage in normal conversations and even "learn" to interact with specific fans. The best AI influencers are designed as a smart, attractive, quirky, likable (or lovable) person that followers and subscribers can trust.

AI influencers are fabricated using AI-powered image generators and avatar software that allows them to engage in natural language conversations and even allows them to "learn" from social interactions. They can be entirely artificial, or they can be an AI version of a real person—which raises the possibility of real people creating virtual versions of themselves that could live on and even keep learning, after they die. Could this be a form of digital immortality?

Some virtual influencers that exist today—and which are not real—have millions of followers and subscribers and generate substantial profits, making this a new business model that is definitely worth watching.

A CGI-generated avatar named Rozy has secured advertising contracts to promote products for more than 100 sponsors. Rozy was created by a Korean media company (Sidus Studio X), using generative AI. Rozy is portrayed as an attractive 22-year-old Asian girl. This virtual influencer has the potential to generate millions of dollars in advertising fees.

Unfortunately AI influencers aren't always positive or trustworthy. AI influencers have been created to engage in devious practices such as phishing for personal and banking information, hacking phones and laptops, and stealing secret data. Some AI influencers created in the image of attractive women have actually succeeded in getting followers to fall in love with them.

- **Podcasters.** There are many stories of men, women, and children who became millionaires by podcasting their opinions and experiences to legions of followers. They can earn money from crowdfunding campaigns, from "stars" awarded by their fans which are converted into financial premiums paid to the podcasters and bloggers, and from sponsored ads that run on the podcaster's website.

One of the most interesting aspects of the video podcast business model is how podcasters can use ordinary activities to generate large numbers of followers and subscribers who either tune into their online shows every day or receive them as "push videos" on Facebook, Instagram, or other social media.

Many podcasters profit from essentially doing their daily activities. For example, many online cooks earn huge incomes from recording and webcasting themselves preparing lunch or dinner every day for their families. Making money from posting yourself making dinner is definitely a new form of business.

One of my favorite podcasters is Ryan Hale, a 20-something linguist who created an entirely new (and innovative) genre by talking to people from other countries in English and then suddenly switching to their own language such as Chinese, Russian, or Indonesian which he also speaks fluently. His YouTube podcast attracted 1.2 million subscribers and became one of the most fun and entertaining podcasts on the Internet.

Cooking podcasts really took off during the pandemic when stay-at-home families were doing more cooking and had time to explore recipes online and cooking podcasts. Some of the most popular include Cooking With Shereen (730,000 subscribers), My Healthy Dish (My Nguyen/two million followers), and Souped Up Recipes (Mandy Manli/1.6 million subscribers). There are also many travel podcasts. A good example is Tangerine Travels (Jordan and May Rusche/290,000 subscribers) which gives tips on traveling and living and Mexico.

- **On-Demand Service Providers.** During the pandemic, everyone needed to be able to get food, groceries, and other items delivered to our door, and this gave impetus to local delivery services with fun names like Uber, DoorDash, and Grubhub. All of these examples and more received a huge boost from the special needs imposed by the pandemic, which have carried over into the post-pandemic NeoWorld. These service providers are continuing to innovate. For example, Uber has been testing the use of autonomous vehicles, also called "robotic taxis."

These are only a few of the new types of organizations and businesses that are being created in the NeoWorld.

Part IV

Neo-Trends

One day I was sitting at a counter in a diner having lunch with my mentor, Jack Tramiel, who was a Holocaust survivor.

"How do you deal with the memories of Auschwitz?" I asked.

Without hesitation Jack replied, "I live in the future."

At that moment, I adopted "living in the future" as my own life-motto—which for me means immersing myself in the future by creating and launching innovations that will make the future happen faster and help improve the world.

8

Living in the Future

The changes imposed by the NeoWorld have forced us to reimagine the future and rethink almost everything. As Neo-Innovators, this means we need to work extra hard to anticipate what's needed and what's possible, in the *future*. What's *needed* in the future could be the solution to a problem, or it could be a new opportunity that needs to be developed and commercialized. What's *possible* can be anything we can imagine.

When we think about innovation, we typically think about something that is totally new. However, the concept of what's "new" is relative. What already exists in one country or market may in fact be totally new in another market where it hasn't been introduced yet. Innovation can include taking a product or service that is already common in one part of the world and making it available to another part of the world that doesn't have access to it yet.

How One Man Changed the Future of Africa One of my favorite innovation stories is how Dr. Mo Ibrahim brought wireless telephone systems to sub-Saharan Africa. In 1998, Dr. Ibrahim noted that Africa was connected by inefficient landlines. Many cities and towns, even the

© The Author(s), under exclusive license to Springer Nature Switzerland AG 2024
M. S. Tomczyk, *Neo-Innovation*, Business Guides on the Go,
https://doi.org/10.1007/978-3-031-74303-0_8

capitals of some countries, weren't even connected. To place a call from some cities, the call had to be routed to Europe and back to the destination city.

Dr. Ibrahim negotiated favorable deals for the rights to modern cellphone technologies used in the United States and Europe and brought them to Africa through his company, Celtel. Within a short time, most of Africa had modern wireless telecommunications, which bypassed the obsolete wireline system and connected the entire continent.

This one innovation—bringing wireless phones to Africa—had enormous impact and lots of side benefits. Dr. Ibrahim did not limit his work to installing networks. He also pioneered banking innovations that allowed people to obtain small "micro-loans" so they could buy cellphones and other essential items. In some rural areas that were very poor financially, an entrepreneur—often a lady in a village called a "cellphone lady"—would buy one cellphone and rent time on the phone so everyone in the village could have access.

Before Africa went wireless, some unscrupulous buyers of crops would visit villages and force farmers to accept whatever prices they offered. This changed when farmers got "connected." Now they could call agricultural crop exchanges in large cities to find out what the current fair price is for any food crop or commodity. This is a great example of how simply moving one radical innovation from one region to another can help improve the world.

Many People Know What's Needed but Don't Know What's Possible When we talk about what's needed as part of the innovation process, we should recognize that not everyone knows what's needed. Often, we don't know we need something until someone invents it.

For example, a lot of people never imagined a world where everyone is glued to their smartphones. Most people thought laptops would shrink and evolve into handheld computers like Apple iPads, but then cellphones evolved into smartphones. For many of us, our phones became our laptops. Apple recognized this when they added iPhones to their product mix. Smartphones also morphed into handheld TV sets, digital cameras, social networking ports, mobile banks, and much more.

If we want to predict the next smartphone, or video doorbell, or air fryer, we can begin by asking "what's needed?" and then ask "what's possible?" even if we don't always know what we need or what's possible.

In past decades, companies would ask customers and users what they think they need, to provide ideas for new products and features. However, as Harvard Professor Clay Christensen noted in his book *The Innovator's Dilemma*, asking existing customers what's needed today often doesn't work because the customers will base their responses on what they know is possible today. Customers typically don't know what's possible because lots of innovations are being developed out of sight, in a research lab, or maybe in an entrepreneur's garage or dorm room.

Neo-Innovators Learn to Read the Future   If you want to create the future or make the future happen faster, you have to live in the future. That means eating, sleeping, and dreaming about what's coming, constantly trying to figure out what's needed and what's possible.

Some people think it's difficult or impossible to predict the future. Actually, there are ways to see the future before it arrives. You can scan the horizon. You can visualize scenarios that haven't happened yet. You can learn what visionaries predict in books and videos. You can track the progress of pilot programs and tests.

Most of the Neo-Innovations that are going to change the world in the future are visible today. I believe that most game-changing innovations exist somewhere in the world today. Sometimes they exist in a laboratory, and sometimes they exist only in a sci-fi novel or movie, but most future innovations exist *somewhere.* The trick is to find them.

Sometimes it's necessary to wait for a gatekeeper technology to be completed to open the door to a solution. In the semiconductor industry during the 1990s, computer and mobile phone developers had to wait for nanocircuits to be developed and commercialized. Nanocircuits provided the capacity needed to turn cellphones into smartphones, make search engines bigger and faster, and create sophisticated innovations like drones, GPS navigation apps, and other data-intensive technologies.

Tomorrow's medical breakthroughs may also be difficult to see today, but we can get a head start by monitoring clinical trials and lab tests. It may take years to complete a clinical trial and more time to test and commercialize the results and secure government approvals, but we can often see tomorrow's medical innovations today, by reading clinical trial reports and updates. This allows us to devote more resources to treatments and cures we want and need but which may be taking a long time to commercialize.

Innovation Maps Help Us Understand What's Possible Innovation maps can be used to map emerging trends as well as technologies, applications, and markets. When creating an innovation map, it's important to think in terms of the entire ecosystem, not just new ideas or inventions.

Think about how various innovations will change customer behaviors, patterns of adoption, pricing and economics, market opportunities, and supply chain management. Think about all the interactions with other areas of science or technology. Consider the impact on different markets and geographic regions. Which killer apps will accelerate market adoption? Think about the value you want to create. Is the value financial or functional? It also helps to design the map so online viewers can click on keywords to view articles, reports, and images.

Here is an innovation map I created to identify the 12 NeoTrends discussed in this section (Fig. 8.1):

Defining the Value Proposition(s) When creating a goal or target for the future, it helps to start with a value proposition. Instead of asking how we can create an innovation, you might start by asking, what would be the value of combining these different technologies and applications? How can we solve problems that exist now or problems that we know are going to exist in the future?

For example, we know that climate change is going to continue to pose problems for the world and for civilization in general. What is the value proposition for a climate change solution? Is the goal to prevent climate change or to adapt to it?

If we decide that we need more innovations like net zero buildings or electric cars, how can we incentivize manufacturers and entrepreneurs to work on these needs, and how can we make it easier to fund and conduct

AGING & LONGEVITY
(Aging Will Become A Treatable Condition)

BRAIN-MACHINE INTERFACE
(Neuralink=Mobility, Telepathy and Telekinesis)

DRONES
(Look, in the Sky, it's a bird, it's a plane, it's a...DRONE!)

AUTONOMOUS VEHICLES
(Self-Driving Vehicles Are On the Road)

NEO-WARS
(Future Wars Will Be Won With Neo-Weapons)

CURING DISEASE
(Chronic and Fatal Diseases Will Become Curable)

Neo-Trends

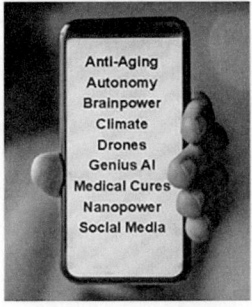

Anti-Aging
Autonomy
Brainpower
Climate
Drones
Genius AI
Medical Cures
Nanopower
Social Media

CLIMATE INNOVATION
(Slowing and Adapting to Climate Change)

ROBOTS
(Jump-Starting the "Robot Revolution")

ARTIFICIAL INTELLIGENCE
(Generative AI Is Making Everything Smarter Than Ever)

WEARABLE COMPUTERS
(Exoskeletons and Exo-Suits)

NANOINNOVATION
(Think Small to Get Big Results)

SPACE EXPLORATION
(Colonizing Mars and Beyond)

Fig. 8.1 This innovation map shows 12 emerging technologies that are already redefining the future and establishing new trends. (Source: M. Tomczyk)

research? How can companies and investors be encouraged to invest in high-risk, long-term innovation projects that may take a decade or more to develop and commercialize?

Prioritizing Innovation Targets Innovations should be ranked and pursued in order of importance, and that means assigning priorities. You may rank your targets by interest or experience, areas where you want to work, or where you might be most qualified. These can also be ranked by short- or long-term time horizons. A 10- or 20-year horizon will require more patience and commitment. Short-term targets are often driven by the potential to create new products and markets to generate income. The best corporations and government agencies work on short-term innovations to maintain momentum but also devote resources to long-term innovations that provide a stake in the future.

9

Neo-Trends That Are Reshaping the Future

If we want to see what the NeoWorld will look like in 10 or 20 years, it helps to look at some major trends that are expected to significantly impact the world. Successful innovators are constantly scanning the near horizon and also the far horizon.

If you think the future is mostly unknown, guess again. It's possible to envision the future and even possible to "scan" it. Most of the radical and disruptive innovations that will create (or change) the future are visible today. Think in terms of what's needed and what's possible, and the future will reveal itself.

Here are a dozen NeoTrends that are already reshaping the future, including an overview of each trend, what's needed and what's possible, and some projects and prototypes being developed now that give a hint of what we might expect and hopefully achieve in the future.

© The Author(s), under exclusive license to Springer Nature Switzerland AG 2024
M. S. Tomczyk, *Neo-Innovation*, Business Guides on the Go,
https://doi.org/10.1007/978-3-031-74303-0_9

Neo-Medicine

More Medical Innovations Are Needed to Cure Disease

Many diseases that were once incurable like HIV/AIDS, some forms of cancer, and heart conditions are now considered "chronic conditions" which means they are treatable but not curable. Some diseases like cholera, tuberculosis, and malaria are now curable, but people continue to die because they do not have access to treatments. COVID-19 is preventable using vaccines and quarantines, but the virus is still not curable. Many diseases will be cured in the next few decades, but new diseases are constantly emerging and developing resistance to cures, so medical innovation is a never-ending process.

The accompanying impact map shows some of the emerging technologies and applications that are being used to treat and cure disease in the NeoWorld. All of these solutions have seen impressive gains in science and research, but most have struggled to move from research to medical practice, which means many cures that have great potential aren't yet approved or available (Fig. 9.1).

There are many reasons for the slow path from research to practice. To begin with, biopharmaceutical firms are not financially incentivized to provide one-time cures that eliminate a disease. They receive most of their compensation from selling drugs that need to be taken for months or years and from long-term therapies. A drug or gene therapy that cures a disease in one visit or prevents a disease forever essentially cuts or minimizes the profits from treating a recurring disease. Some orphan diseases may never be cured unless government subsidies or charitable contributions are provided.

Many diseases are complex and require expensive diagnostic tests to detect. This means that we need less expensive tests for complicated diseases, especially conditions involving genes, proteins, and chromosomes. DNA/gene testing should be a routine medical test for everyone, but these tests are still very expensive and need to be cost-reduced so everyone can afford them.

GENE THERAPY

Disease causing genes can be replaced, deleted or repaired—but gene therapy is complex, expensive and not yet

GENE EDITING

CRISPR is a successful gene editing tool that allows genes to be edited like software is edited by programmers.

CUSTOM VACCINES

Vaccines help prevent COVID, Papillomavirus, Hepatitis B and influenza. Personalized (neoantigen) vaccines train T cells to prevent and fight specific tumors & other diseases.

ROBOTIC SURGERY

Robotic surgeons are performing micro-surgery.

CURING DISEASE

MOST major diseases are NOT cured. Cancer accounts for one of every 6 deaths worldwide. Better diagnostics & custom therapies are needed.

NEO
Medicine

AGE SLOWING SOLUTIONS

Aging is becoming a treatable condition—healthspan & lifespan can be increased.

REPLACEMENT THERAPIES

Stem cell, bone marrow transplants and organ transplants are common.

Parents are experimenting with receiving "young blood" from their children.

Organ transplants have the potential to "grow your own replacement organs.

NANOMEDICINE

Nanocarriers deliver drugs & proteins to treat & prevent disease.

Nanosizing drugs allow them to penetrate cell walls & membranes.

Disease fighting nano-bots are being tested.

DNA DIAGNOSTICS

The combination of fast affordable DNA testing and gene editing is poised to transform the entire field of medicine.

Fig. 9.1 If we combine Neo and medicine to create Neo-Medicine, this helps us think about a new era of medicine which we can begin to describe in an innovation map like this one. (Source: M. Tomczyk)

Treatments requiring organ transplants or gene therapies can cost as much as $1 million or more which means they are not available to everyone. Many chemotherapies and gene therapy solutions don't last long because the body adjusts and rejects them. Also, some genetic diseases are caused by several different genes, not just one, which complicates diagnosis and treatment. Ideally, we need to develop affordable, effective treatments that can be customized to individual patients.

Despite many scientific advances, the record for delivering medical cures to patients has *not* been great. In the past few decades, there has been a startling increase in cancer. Cancers in people under 50 have increased almost 80% worldwide. The causes have been attributed to food additives and "forever" chemicals in water and packaging, and there is new research that suggests obesity may be a factor.

Scientific advances have given us the ability to understand and treat many diseases, but the reality is we still can't cure most diseases. Also, the causes of many diseases are still hidden. The need for innovation in the medical field is urgent and potentially affects all of us.

What's Needed are new and better therapies, treatments, and cures for heart disease, stroke, Alzheimer's/dementia, liver disease, muscular dystrophy, Parkinson's, Huntington's disease, and more than 200 forms of cancer.

The need for medical treatments and cures is serious and profound. The best way to illustrate the need for medical Neo-Innovations is to list the medical conditions that still *cannot* be cured, despite decades of intense medical research.

The cost of health treatments is enormous, and the cost in human suffering is incalculable. We need new and better ways to prevent diseases, infections, and inherited conditions. We need to develop faster, more accurate, ideally noninvasive methods to detect and diagnose medical conditions before symptoms develop. We need to cure diseases that are currently still incurable and often fatal.

Here are some examples of diseases and medical conditions where new approaches are needed:

- **Cancer.** A few forms of cancer have been "cured" by the introduction of vaccines, but the number of cancers that are still not curable is overwhelming. This is because there are more than 200 separate forms of cancer and many subcategories caused by genetic mutations that are difficult to diagnose. In addition, cancer cells in the same tumor may have different genetic mutations. Cancer cells can also develop resistance or immunity to treatments over time requiring new or modified versions of drugs. Also, cancer cells do not have normal cell mechanisms that prevent cells from growing or dividing, which allows many cancers to spread to many organs.
- **Mosquito-Borne Diseases.** Mosquitoes can transmit more than half a dozen diseases that are mostly incurable. These include malaria, zika,

dengue fever, West Nile virus, and yellow fever. More than 247 million cases of malaria occur each year, and over 620,000 people die each year from this mosquito-transmitted disease. Most of the victims are children under the age of five, and most cases occur in Africa, where 40% of the public health budget in some countries is spent treating malaria. In addition to vaccines and repellants, innovative solutions include genetically modifying mosquito species to wipe out the species responsible for specific diseases.

- **Heart Disease.** The leading cause of death in the world is heart disease. In the United States, someone dies every 33 s from cardiovascular disease. A large percentage of premature deaths are caused by heart disease. We need to find ways to prevent and cure heart disease, to save lives, to reduce healthcare and insurance costs, and to increase our lifespans.
- **Alzheimer's Disease.** In the United States, one person develops Alzheimer's disease every 65 s, and more than 10% of Americans over 65 suffer from this debilitating disease. There are approximately 700,000 cases just in California. Over 70% of Alzheimer's cases affect people aged 75 and older, which means if we want to increase our health span and lifespan, we need to find ways to prevent or cure Alzheimer's. It is possible that a solution may involve gene editing. For example, researchers have discovered that more than half of Alzheimer's patients have at least one copy of the APOE-e4 gene. We also need to understand specifically how these biological processes occur. We know that this disease results from an accumulation of tau proteins and damaged neurons, but how do we prevent these processes?
- **Autism.** One of the greatest needs in the field of medicine involves autism, which has been increasing at an alarming rate during the past two decades. In 2023 the Centers for Disease Control reported that 1 in 36 children is now diagnosed with autism, up from 1 in 44 only 2 years before. During the 1970s, only 4 or 5 children out of every 10,000 developed autism, and by 2025 more than half of all children are expected to contract it. The timing of this dramatic increase suggests that something in food or packaging may be responsible, and research suggests that one possible cause could be an additive such as

bisphenol A (BPA) which is used in plastics. Medical innovators need to explore more possibilities because the need is urgent.

- **Environmental Diseases.** Many medical conditions are caused by exposure to pollutants and hazardous chemicals in the environment. For example, virtually every source of water in the United States is contaminated with what are known as "forever chemicals"—disease-causing chemicals that persist in the environment for decades or even centuries. In addition to treating pollution-related illnesses, we should find better ways to tackle pollution at the source. It doesn't make sense to treat people who get sick from environmental mistakes when the "cure" is to prevent the pollution *before* people get sick.
- **Genetic Disorders.** We need to improve gene editing so we can add, remove, or replace genes associated with causing or curing disease. As previously discussed we need to find better ways to extend our lifespan and our health span.

The healthcare community needs better diagnostic tools to detect, diagnose, treat, and cure all types of diseases and medical conditions. Physicians, surgeons, and medical care facilities need to adopt a more holistic approach that incorporates all of the technologies that exist today. We also need to be able to gain emergency access to therapies that are experimental and/or in clinical trials.

Expanding the Medical Ecosystem In the NeoWorld, the medical ecosystem is being redefined to include (and make available and affordable) all relevant tests, treatments, therapies, and cures, as well as access to input from disease advocacy groups and patient communities.

Here is an infographic called the *INTEGRATE* model developed by a team of Australian and UK researchers that shows what a comprehensive disease prevention, detection, treatment, and cure "map" might look like. The *INTEGRATE* model seeks to combine polygenic genomic and diagnostic testing and history data for target chronic illnesses to identify subpopulations that are low risk, at risk, and with diagnosed and undiagnosed conditions. Every box on this diagram is a potential area for Neo-Innovation (Fig. 9.2).

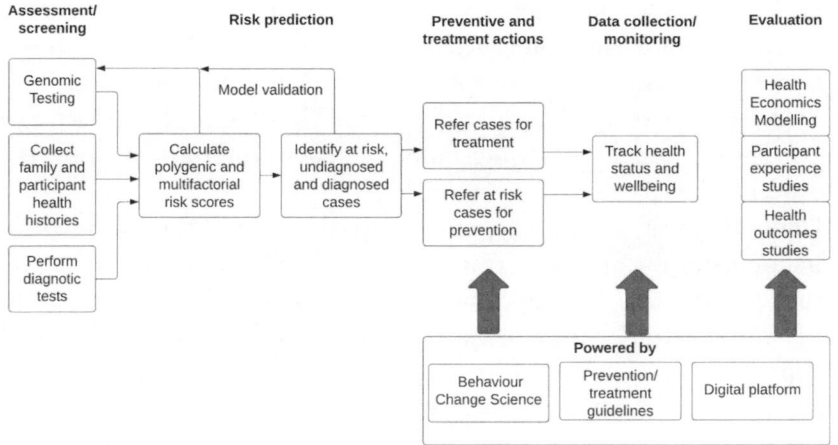

Fig. 9.2 This framework—called *INTEGRATE*—was developed by a team of Australian and UK researchers to map the interactions between disease prevention, detection, treatment, and cure. (Copyright © 2023 Thomas, Browning, Charchar, Klein, Ory, Bowden-Jones and Chamberlain. Source: Frontiers in Public Health; 13 October 2023. Open Source illustration)

What's Possible Modern medical solutions include preventive measures, diagnostic tests, and treatments that can slow or stabilize a disease, as well as permanent cures. The technologies and applications that make these solutions possible include new types of CT and MRI scans, better tests to identify genes and proteins that can create or cure diseases, and commercialization of gene editing techniques that will allow us to add, delete, or replace genes that can cause or cure diseases.

Following are some "Neo-Medicine" examples which you may want to monitor, since your health and life in the future and the well-being of your friends and family may depend on one or more of these medical technologies:

- **Cancer** is typically treated with chemotherapy and drugs; however, most cancers are still incurable. Only two cancer vaccines exist, for HPV and hepatitis B. A few promising therapies such as cancer-fighting monoclonal antibodies are in clinical trials, and some therapies are beginning to show results.

An injectable life-extending immunotherapy called atezolizumab (Tecentriq®) is an immune checkpoint inhibitor that can strengthen a patient's immune system to specifically seek and destroy cancer cells. This drug works by binding to the protein PD-L1 on the surface of a cancer cell, which allows the immune system to attack and kill the cancer cell.

- **Gene therapy** was developed during the mid-1990s to identify, manipulate, repair, and replace disease-related genes. The first gene therapy (Kymriah, a leukemia treatment) was not approved by the FDA until 2017. Today, about 30 gene and cell therapies have been approved by the FDA. Most gene therapies are still in clinical trials, and commercialization has been extremely slow.

- **Gene editing** is a more recent form of gene therapy that hopes to provide the ability to edit human, animal, and plant genomes like we use word processing to edit software. Some gene editing tools such as CRSPR are so easy to use that they are being used in classroom experiments to teach gene therapy and genetic engineering to high school students. Other forms of gene editing are being developed. Diseases caused by a single defective (or missing) gene are probably the first that will be cured by gene editing. Polygenic conditions that result from interactions between multiple genes will take longer to cure.

- **New types of vaccines for malaria and other diseases**. Molecular medicine has given us the ability to view and study biological processes even at the nanoscale where viruses and other biological structures exist. This is a prime area for medical innovation in the new era. The first malaria vaccine (RTS,S) was created by GlaxoSmithKline and approved by the World Health Organization in 2021. It has been administered to more than two million children in Africa, and a second vaccine (R21/Matrix-M) has been approved. These vaccines could potentially save tens of thousands of lives. This is an exciting development; however, better methods for distributing malaria vaccines are needed especially to people in remote and rural areas where malaria is most prevalent.

- **Molecular medicine** treats diseases at the cell level, instead of treating tissues and organs. Scientists are learning how to create smaller versions of drug molecules that can enter and destroy cancer cells inside individual tumor cells and are experimenting with "carriers" that can be used to transport disease-fighting proteins to targeted cells.
- **Nanomedicine** is a form of molecular medicine that treats disease by studying and manipulating biological structures and processes that are too small to see with an optical microscope, such as genes and DNA. Some drug molecules that are proven to fight cancer are too large to pass through the walls of human cells, so they need to be "nano-sized" so they can enter targeted cells. The good news is that it is possible to nano-size cancer-fighting molecules, and it is also possible to engineer nano-carriers to transport drugs in the human body. It is also possible to use proteins to target and help destroy specific cancer cells.
- **Regenerative medicine** uses stem cells to grow replacement tissues and organs. Dr. Anthony Atala, the first surgeon to successful grow and implant a human organ (a human bladder) from a patient's own cells, is a pioneer in this field. Dr. Atala at Wake Forest University has proven that it is possible to grow tissues and organs. After achieving some success growing basic organs like bladders, he and his team have been working to develop ways to grow denser more complex organs like the heart and liver. In the future it will be possible to "grow our own organs" to replace defective or damaged organs.

Wellness Medicine One of the most intriguing trends in Neo-Medicine is the growth of "wellness" practices like MDVIP that focus on the prevention of disease and development of antiaging treatments and ways to extend our health span (how long we stay healthy) as well as our lifespan. Many doctors are beginning to provide supplements, drugs, and lifestyle recommendations to treat aging like any medical condition. That doesn't mean we can cure aging and live forever, but it definitely means we can slow the aging process and add "bonus decades" to our lives.

Aging and Longevity

Aging Will Become a Treatable Condition

Scientists now believe that for some people in their 80s and 90s, their biological age is decades younger than their chronological age. They also believe it is possible to engineer this result through the right combination of diet, exercise, fasting, weight control, and lifestyle. A major goal for medical Neo-Innovators is to be able to treat aging like we treat any disease.

Medical researchers are actively researching how to slow the aging process and keep us healthier longer. The goal is to redefine aging as a treatable condition. Many scientists now believe that the right combination of medical and lifestyle innovations can extend the human lifespan from the current average of 73–79 years to 100–110 years. There are many signs that this notion is gaining momentum and traction. In October 2023, *The Economist* published a special issue on aging with three simple but powerful words on the cover: "LIVING TO 120."

We can think about slowing the aging process, but if we can actually accomplish that, it also means that we could effectively delay the onset of death itself. There is a wonderful stage play called "Death Takes a Holiday." This fanciful concept is actually becoming a possibility. In the real world, death is inevitable, but in the NeoWorld, it may be possible to *delay* death. We can in theory force death to "take a holiday" and give ourselves some bonus decades by changing our lifestyles and how we practice medicine.

What's Needed One of the goals of medical research is to find ways to achieve longer healthier lives. To extend our longevity, we need to develop new and better ways to (1) slow the aging process, (2) extend our health spans (staying healthy longer), and (3) redefine aging as a treatable condition like any disease.

If we want to extend our lifespan, we also need to find ways to extend our *health span* which means keeping people healthier longer. This goes hand in hand with slowing the aging process. If we live longer, we also have to be able to stay healthier longer because it doesn't make sense to live longer if living longer means becoming feeble, incapacitated, or demented. Treating older patients, in their 80s, 90s and 100s can be expensive and burdensome, so part of the value proposition to age-related solutions should include developing ways to reduce the cost of these medical treatments.

What's Possible It is possible to live to 110 or 120. Some people are living that long now, so we know this is possible. The question is, what do we need to change if we want to live past 100?

Current research suggests it's possible to extend our lifespan if we can (1) change medical practice from primary care to wellness care, (2) identify and use gene editing to give long-life genes to anyone, and (3) learn how to mimic and recreate the conditions that allow Blue Zone communities to routinely live past 100.

Scientists are actively studying Blue Zones[1] where a large percent of people routinely live past 100. These "longevity pockets" include communities in a dozen places around the world including Sardinia, Italy; Ikaria, Greece; Okinawa, Japan; Costa Rica's Nicoya Peninsula; and Loma Linda, California. It is believed that replicating the lifestyle, diet, and daily activities of these centenarians can teach us how to turn cities and towns into Blue Zone communities.

Can lifestyle changes and medical treatments really give us a longer life? In his book, *Outlive: The Science and Art of Longevity*,[2] Dr. Peter Attia suggests that we all have the ability to gain two or three "bonus decades"—remaining healthy in our 80s and 90s and even past 100, if we take age-slowing supplements and drugs, optimize how we exercise and sleep, and stay active.

Medical studies have shown that the diabetes drug metformin and the supplement berberine have the potential to slow aging. As age-slowing

---

[1] Buettner, Dan; The Blue Zones Secrets for Living Longer: Lessons From the Healthiest Places on Earth; Geographic, 2023.
[2] Attia, Peter; Outlive: The Science and Art of Longevity; Harmony Books; 2023.

drugs are confirmed by clinical trials, it is likely that we will see drugs being prescribed to treat aging like we treat any disease.

Neo-Innovations Underway Now Here are some of the most interesting age-slowing approaches that are underway now. These longevity programs are redefining how we define and treat aging:

- **Age-Slowing Research.** A notable example of longevity research is Northwestern University's study of "superagers"—people in their 80s who retain the mental acuity and physical health of people decades younger. Another leader in antiaging research is the SENS Research Organization, a nonprofit group that sponsors and promotes new medical therapies to treat age-related diseases.
- **Physicians Are Practicing "Wellness."** In the past decade, a growing number of primary care physicians have converted to "wellness" practices. This coincides with recent guidance from the World Health Organization which now defines health as "A state of optimal well-being, not merely the absence of disease and infirmity." This is a radical change from the traditional view of medicine which focused on treating or curing medical conditions based on patient symptoms and lab tests.

    Medical wellness is a holistic approach that involves treating all the factors that contribute to personal well-being including physical, mental, emotional, environmental, spiritual, and social components.

    Today, wellness practitioners are administering detailed blood, urine, heart, and organ tests to identify early signals that a patient might be susceptible to heart disease, diabetes, Alzheimer's, other medical conditions. One of the largest wellness programs is called MDVIP. Patients pay an annual fee to receive special tests in addition to normal physical exams that reveal deficiencies in blood sugar, cholesterol, cardiac health, as well as levels of proteins, hormones, and blood components that may signal current and future health risks. Patients may be given supplements or drugs to correct any deficiencies before they grow serious. For example, a statin may be prescribed to prevent or treat plaque forming in heart valves and arteries.

A wellness blood test may reveal that someone who doesn't spend enough time in the sun has a vitamin D deficiency in which case the doctor may suggest taking a daily vitamin D3 supplement. Clinical studies have shown that patients who are deficient in vitamin D have a higher likelihood of contracting COVID and also a higher probability of life-threatening symptoms. Scientists have also found that taking vitamin D can help protect against COVID infections.

- **Learning the Secrets of Superagers.** Researchers at Northwestern University, Harvard Medical School, and other universities are working to unlock the secrets of people in their 80s and 90s who have the mental acuity and physical health of people whose biological age seems to be much younger than their chronological age. Northwestern University has begun to identify why some superagers develop Alzheimer's disease, while others do not.

Some studies have shown that people in their 80s who exercise at high intensity for 20–45 min daily have an aerobic capacity of people 30 years younger, according to Dr. J. Andrew Taylor, director of the Cardiovascular Research Laboratory at the Harvard-affiliated Spaulding Rehabilitation Network in Boston.[3] Researchers believe that regular exercise reduces many age-related risks.

In 2015, more than 4000 participants in the 14th National Senior Games in Baton Rouge, Louisiana, took a "fitness age" survey developed by researchers at the Norwegian University of Science and Technology in Trondheim, Norway. The surveys revealed that the average chronological age of the participants was 68, but their average biological age was 43. The Norwegian researchers also found that older people who are "fit" tend to have lower waist sizes, higher aerobic capacity (known as VO_2), and active lifestyles.

We know that superagers exist because there are more than half a dozen places in the world where people routinely live past 100 and stay healthy throughout their long lives. The challenge is to turn the secrets of these centenarians into age-slowing treatments and therapies.

---

[3] Harvard Health Publishing, What does it take to be a super-ager?; Harvard Medical School; 1 May 2017.

- **Community and Personal Blue Zones.** More than half a dozen communities in the world have been designated "Blue Zones." These are places where people routinely live past 100 and stay healthy throughout their long lives. Blue Zone communities are located in Sardinia, Italy; the Nicoya Peninsula in Costa Rica; the Greek island of Icaria; a religious community in Loma Linda, California; and in the city state of Singapore. The existence of these communities begs the question, what if we could learn their long life secrets and apply them like a recipe to enable most people to live past 100?

  Blue Zone communities were originally discovered in a demographic study by Dr. Michel Poulain, a professor at the University of Sassari in Italy, and Dr. Gianni Pes, a Belgian demographer, and popularized by National Geographic explorer Dan Buettner. Dan trademarked the name Blue Zones˚ and created a project to study and replicate the habits, diets, and lifestyles of people who live in Blue Zone communities. The goal is to commercialize Blue Zones by creating programs that any neighborhood, community, or town can use to increase the health span and lifespan of its residents.

- **Recipes for a Longer Life.** Based on current research on aging and longevity, we are beginning to see "long life recipes" that we can actually apply to stay healthier and live longer. These suggestions will keep changing and evolving as research keeps revealing and fine-tuning the best antiaging solutions. Here are some age-slowing approaches recommended by various experts and organizations:

(a) Keep moving (walk or power walk, jog, use a treadmill, hike, stay active)
(b) Minimize stress
(c) Eat less (strive to maintain healthy weight levels)
(d) Eat healthy (more vegetables and less sugar, salt, and unsaturated fat)
(e) Fast periodically
(f) Get enough sleep
(g) Have faith (the overwhelming majority of centenarians are religious)
(h) Participate in social groups and communities
(i) Eliminate known health risks (smoking, drinking, taking drugs)

(j) Take age-slowing drugs and supplements (metformin, a diabetes drug, and berberine, a glucose control supplement, have been shown to slow aging; more are being studied)

It will be interesting to see in the coming decades if Ray Kurzweil and other futurists were correct in predicting that eventually we will develop ways to live to 110 or 120 and perhaps even "forever."

Robots

Jump-Starting the "Robot Revolution"

One of the hallmarks of the NeoWorld is the rise of smart machines, especially the smartest machine which is the *robot*. Robots are poised to change the world. However, they are still not user-friendly, mobile, or affordable enough to become mass market appliances.

Here's a short poem I wrote that describes the current status of robots:

> *Robots and Androids and Cyborgs and More!*
> *Most of them can't even open a door.*
> *It's really hard to find a good robot store.*
> *Most of us don't know what robots are for,*
> *unless it's a factory where robots abound.*
> *or the surface of Mars where rovers are found.*
> *But if we keep going we'll figure it out.*
> *And then maybe robots will give us a shout,*
> *to tell us themselves what they're really all about.*

A *robot* is a device that resembles a living creature and can move independently to perform tasks and interact with its environment. It can be programmed to perform repetitive tasks like a mechanical arm in a factory, or it can be a humanoid device that looks, acts, communicates, and "learns" like a real person.

The most common robots in use today are industrial robots. Most are programmable manipulators that can operate on three or more axes. There are 20 million industrial robots in use today. More than 200,000 industrial robots are in use at Amazon as part of the company's stream-lined supply chain. Some Amazon transport robots carry 8-foot-tall shelves loaded with packages and travel 10 miles or more every day. Amazon robots have allowed warehouses and fulfillment centers to process four times more packages than before robots were installed, although robots still aren't able to grasp as many different types and shapes of packages as human workers. Amazon predicts that robotic grasping technology will catch up to human capabilities by 2030 (Fig. 9.3).

High-level robots can operate autonomously and can be designed in human form. *Humanoid robots* have human features although most humanoids today still have faces that look "alien" with eyes shaped like orbs or slits. Some have legs that look like jointed pins. Others are shaped like people but move on wheels instead of legs. Some humanoids are designed to look "human" but look mostly like department store manikins.

Fig. 9.3 Automated transport robots deliver stacked modules to human workers at Amazon fulfillment centers. (Source: Amazon Press Center)

The highest level of humanoid robot is an *android*, which is a robot that is so realistic it could pass for a real human. Scientists are engineering androids that act like real people, and some inventors have designed robots that look like themselves.

Thanks to generative AI, machine learning, and other emerging technologies, robots are getting smarter. Most humanoid robots are interactive, can converse in natural language, read human facial expressions, and react to emotions (Fig. 9.4).

What's Needed Every innovation needs a killer application that catches the imagination of the mass market and provides a reason to buy it. The killer applications for humanoid robots have yet to be clearly defined although several applications are being tested.

In a practical sense, we need to know, what are the functional reasons for designing humanoids with faces, arms, legs, eyes, ears, etc.? Does a robot really need to look human? Which applications require a human

Fig. 9.4 The first generation of interactive robots look like cartoon characters and were mostly designed for entertainment and customer service/PR purposes. Left to right: Atlas by Boston Dynamics, Pepper (Softbank/Aldebaran Robotics), and Nao (Aldebaran). Boston Dynamics claims that their acrobatic robot (Atlas) is the world's most dynamic humanoid robot. (Source: iStock)

appearance, and which don't require human features? Matching form and function is a major challenge for all robotic engineers.

Humanoid robots are intriguing, we can all agree on that. But what practical, cost-effective functions will humanoid robots perform? Sometimes we invent things before we know their true purpose. So it is with humanoid robots.

Most current applications have been called "companion robots," and these are mostly novelties. Robots are being tested in customer service roles to answer customer questions in places like Home Depot stores. During the pandemic, humanoid receptionists were considered to be a possible application, for use in hospitals and office buildings to greet and interact with people who might potentially be infected with COVID.

Some robots are used today in hazardous environments such as dealing with armed criminals and rescuing people from hazardous locations where fire, flooding, chemical leaks, and explosive materials pose risks to prevent human rescuers and first responders. Better designs are needed to make these first responder bots more affordable and functional.

What's needed is a robot with the right price/performance and a killer application that will jump-start the robot revolution (Fig. 9.5).

What's Possible Humanoid robots are clearly moving from science fiction to science reality. Thanks to advances in several compatible technologies, it is now possible to design humanoid robots that resemble and closely mimic in every way their creators, as well as celebrities and customers who want to create robots in their own image.

These robots can capture mannerisms, personality quirks, voice patterns, and more. Some robots can read faces and interpret facial expressions, which they respond to with a form of artificial empathy. Ishiguro Labs are testing "telepresence robots" which are humanoid replicants of real people that can attend meetings and autonomous social robots that can communicate with groups of people in social situations and environments.

Robots can learn from conversations and experiences, and deep learning AI allows a robot to learn on its own. Robots equipped with GPS can navigate autonomously.

Fig. 9.5 Left: Dr. Ishiguro with Geminoid™ HI-4 developed by Osaka University and ATR Hiroshi Ishiguro Laboratories. Right: ERICA was introduced in 2015 by the ERATO ISHIGURO Symbiotic Human-Robot Interaction Project. (Photos courtesy of Ishiguro Labs and Osaka University)

Many robots draw their "intelligence" from databases located on cloud servers. Robots need large databases to support natural language communication, engage in conversation, and answer questions (Fig. 9.6). Here are some humanoid robots that exist today:

- **Sophia:** The best known humanoid robot is Sophia, which is also the first robot to be granted citizenship by a nation. Sophia is a humanoid robot developed by Hanson Robotics, a Hong Kong-based company. Sophia uses AI, visual data processing, and facial recognition to conduct humanlike conversations. She was designed to learn and adapt to human behavior, which contributes to her ability to form relationships with humans. Sophia has been granted the title of the world's first robot citizen by Saudi Arabia, and she serves as the United Nations Development Programme's first nonhuman innovation champion.
- **Zeno** is a 2-ft-tall robot boy developed by Hanson Robotics. Zeno is being used to provide treatment to children with autism, in a collaborative research initiative by the University of Texas at Arlington, the Dallas Autism Treatment Center, Texas Instruments and National Instruments, and Hanson Robotics.

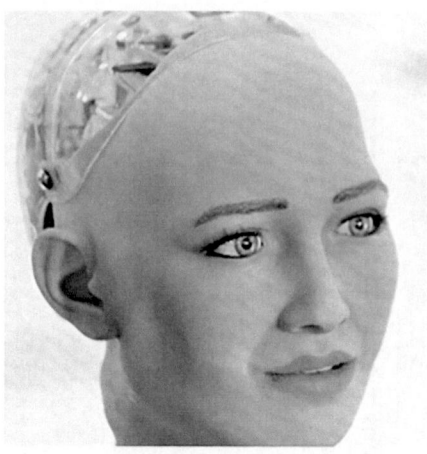

Fig. 9.6 Sophia the robot is a lifelike humanoid robot developed by Hanson Robotics, founded by Dr. David Hanson (*shown here with Sophia*). (Images courtesy of Hanson Robotics)

- **Optimus** is a humanoid robot developed by Elon Musk's robot team at Tesla. Optimus is originally called Tesla Bot. The first prototypes were announced in 2022, and videos showing Optimus doing various activities such as walking, doing yoga, and sorting items by color were shown in September and December 2023. A goal is for Optimus to perform a full range of human tasks. The robot may also have a role on Mars if Musk succeeds in launching space colony missions to the Red Planet. It is notable that "Optimus Prime" is a fictional robot and hero in the *Transformers* movie franchise.
- **Atlas** by Boston Dynamics is the world's most acrobatic robot. Atlas is a four-legged robot with jointed arms and legs that can run, jump, and negotiate different types of terrain. Boston Dynamics' owners include Hyundai (80%) and Softbank (20%).
- **Geminoid**™ is a family of humanoid robots developed by Osaka University, the Advanced Telecommunications Research Institute International (ATR), and Ishiguro Laboratories. The first Geminoid prototypes resemble its cocreator, roboticist Hiroshi Ishiguro, director of the Intelligent Robotics Lab at Osaka University and visiting director at ATR Hiroshi Ishiguro Laboratories. Erica, introduced in 2015

by Ishiguro Labs, is an autonomous conversational android capable of natural interaction.

- **Android Robo-C** is a humanoid service robot that incorporates over 600 lifelike facial expressions. Robo-C was developed by Promobot, the largest robotics company in Russia and Eastern Europe, manufacturing autonomous service robots used in over 30 countries. Customers can specify the appearance and language of the robot. Robo-C robots are in use at airports, trade shows, museums, schools, and shopping malls; they are used as greeters, museum guides, concierges, and administrators.

These are only a few of the dozens of robots being developed around the world. Some other examples include Ameca by Engineered Arts which can detect emotions during human interactions; Alter 3, a musical humanoid created by Osaka University and Mixi; Armar-6, developed by the Karlsruhe Institute of Technology in Germany; Astro, by Apptronik, a "work robot" designed by a spinout from the University of Texas at Austin; and JiaJia, the first Chinese humanoid robot, developed by the University of Science and Technology.

Artificial Intelligence

Generative AI Is Making Everything Smarter Than Ever

In 2022, after decades of development, artificial intelligence (AI) took a giant leap forward. A smarter-than-ever set of algorithms called "generative AI" created smart, interactive, natural language systems that can autonomously search the Internet, retrieve and share information, answer questions, make suggestions, create content, and even write books and articles. Because of their extraordinary communication capabilities, generative AI chatbots are often called large language models (LLMs). This is a huge paradigm shift. It means that artificial intelligence is still artificial but also more "human" than ever before. The implications for the future are profound.

ChatGPT, which stands for Chat Generative Pre-trained Transformer, is an artificial intelligence chatbot launched by OpenAI in November 2022 in collaboration with Microsoft. ChatGPT became the fastest adopted software application in history, garnering over 1 billion users in the first 5 min of its launch. The influence of this AI application on emerging Neo-Innovations is profound and enormously transformative. ChatGPT is already being incorporated as a search engine assistant, content creator, and an AI "brain" for avatars and robots.

Other generative AI examples include Bard by Google, a large language chatbot that has advanced search engine capabilities as well as math, reasoning, and coding capabilities. Bing AI from Microsoft is powered by OpenAI's GPT4 and can generate both written and visual content in 100 languages. Apple is also rumored to be developing a chatbot. Dall-E is an implementation of OpenAI's GPT technology that connects the meaning of words to visual elements and allows users to generate imagery in multiple styles.

What's Needed? The rapid advance of chatbot technology came in response to a need for smarter search engines, increased interactivity (stimulated by social media use), and faster Internet access, which enabled the development of smarter AI programs and large language models.

At this early stage in the development of generative AI and intelligent chatbots, innovators need to develop vertical application frameworks that are specific to various functions. For example, an AI chatbot that searches the Internet and delivers a specific answer to a query requires different capabilities from a chatbot that is asked to create content for a report, an ad, or a PowerPoint slide.

A chatbot user may type a simple command like "Write me a sentence on this topic" or "Create an image that shows this information," but the algorithms used to create those different results may be unique, complex, and totally different. This is a reminder that radical innovators are constantly being challenged to create interfaces that are super complicated to design and program but need to look simple, friendly, and ergonomic to the user.

Most generative AI systems are text based. The next generation of AI is expanding the capabilities of chatbots to create and manipulate images making them, essentially, *imagebots.*

Another need involves improving the reliability of AI systems. We need to find better ways to keep AI programs "honest" and prevent trusted AI systems from conveying lies, misinformation, and biased content.

We also need to monitor and control the evolution of sentient (self-aware) machines. In the real world, how we view ourselves and what we call self-awareness can vary widely from person to person. People can be realistic or delusional. Keeping AI systems from becoming "delusional" is a challenge. AI developers need to develop stronger guardrails to keep AI "sane," filter inappropriate responses, and prevent the spread of misinformation.

Giving computerized systems the ability to make independent choices and decisions requires a high degree of trust which means that generative AI developers need to consider ethics, morals, truth, and honesty as part of the development process. Since it has been impossible to keep fake news and bias out of news media that is supposed to be objective, we can expect that building truth and honesty into AI systems will be difficult.

What's Possible? In the AI community, Neo-Innovators are working hard to engineer and perfect a wide variety of applications based on new algorithms, interfaces, and capabilities.

Now and in the future, general and customized AI systems will manage and orchestrate complex tasks such as processing data from space telescopes, tracking weather patterns, monitoring biological processes, interpreting DNA and genome tests, and analyzing and responding to social media viewers and online shoppers, to name a few.

New capabilities to mine data and analyze results quickly are already giving company decision-makers new ways to manage their organizations and turn insights into actions. These capabilities are not fully developed or understood yet, but we can expect AI to become an increasingly powerful management tool. Management consulting firms such as McKinsey,

Cognizant, and others are beginning to develop AI platforms to help clients manage their enterprises.

AI interfaces are just getting started, but we can expect to see a myriad of new types of interfaces that change how we connect, communicate, and collaborate. Today, we are connecting with AI chatbots, smart search engines, and creative bots. In the coming decade, we will be asked to authorize AI systems to contact us by email or text message us just like a human friend, to give us information the AI system "knows" we want or need. This is already happening to some extent as we all know from the constant stream of messages—some unwanted and annoying—that keep appearing on our smartphones.

There is a plethora of opportunities for innovators to apply generative AI capabilities to devices and physical systems that don't have smart chatbots yet, such as neobanking applications, online security, customer service, military systems, autonomous vehicles, navigation services, and giving "personalities" to robots and androids. Generative AI is already making robots and other machines more "human" as well as smarter.

It has been said that one of the defining characteristics of the human species is self-awareness. One of the most intriguing possibilities is the potential for smarter AI systems to provide "sentience" (self-awareness) to computers and robots. Self-aware machines can become valued partners in the innovation process and in society, or they could become threats. A defective AI system could even suffer a form of technological insanity resulting in dangerous or destructive behavior. How to keep AI friendly and not dangerous or destructive is a challenge for AI Neo-Innovators.

Brain-Machine Interface

Neuralink: Mobility, Telepathy, and Telekinesis

Imagine being able to connect our brains to the Internet, the cloud, and to each other like we connect smartphones. Think about the implication of a device that allows us to turn thought into action. This could give us a form of mental telepathy—turning our brains into wireless thought-phones—or telekinesis which is the ability to move objects with our thoughts.

If we can control a computer or other device with our minds, we could establish a link between the brain of a paralyzed accident victim and their arms and legs or with a prosthetic device that allows them to walk and restores their mobility.

Actually this innovation, which certainly sounds radical, is already being developed. And it has a good chance of succeeding because it's being developed by the world's most successful innovator, Elon Musk.

What's Needed? The idea for a brain-machine interface was inspired by a real-world need to provide new ways for paralysis victims and amputees to control bionic limbs and access computers and smartphones and other devices.

There are more than 50 million victims of trauma, paralysis, and amputations in the world today. As many as half a million people are paralyzed every year due to traffic accidents, natural disasters, and wars. Globally, more than one million people suffer limb amputations every year from accidents, wars, and diseases like diabetes or amyotrophic lateral sclerosis (ALS).

Ideally, what's needed is a chip or circuit that can be safely implanted in the brain to provide a wireless connection to a bionic limb, prosthetic, or exoskeleton. If successful, this innovation could help millions of handicapped people regain mobility, walk, drive, and use a computer and smartphone.

What's Possible Now? In 2016 Elon Musk launched a venture called Neuralink to develop a brain-computer interface. Neuralink has been called the world's first "neurotech" company.

Musk challenged his Neuralink team to develop a brain interface using a combination of artificial intelligence, biochemistry, integrated circuits, neuroscience, robotics, and wireless communication. These technologies are being integrated to create a system that can decipher brain signals and transmit them to external devices. They are also designing robotic systems to precisely insert and connect tiny, delicate electrodes. Neuralink's system also includes amplifiers to boost brain signals like boosting a wireless signal to make it more stable and reliable.

The initial goal is to restore mobility and other functions to paralysis victims and amputees by enabling them to control a computer, smartphone, bionic limb/prosthesis, or exoskeleton.

In 2019 Neuralink announced that it was developing a system capable of processing information from neurons, based on technology developed at the University of California-San Francisco and UC-Berkeley. The company has also announced the development of a surgical robot designed to insert Neuralink probes into the brain with minimum tissue damage. The team is also working on a method for converting information obtained from neurons into binary code which can convey instructions to external devices. In May 2023, Neuralink received FDA approval to begin human clinical trials, and in September 2023 the company began recruiting candidates for human patient trials.

In January 2024, Musk announced that the first human patient was implanted with a Neuralink chip. Musk added that the first Neuralink "product" is called Telepathy and will be developed and tested in a 6-year clinical trial. The trial focuses on individuals who have paralysis in all four limbs due to a spinal cord injury or amyotrophic lateral sclerosis (ALS). The goal is to give patients the ability to use thought to control their phone, computer, and other devices.

What's Possible in the Future? Eventually, brain implants will allow paraplegics to walk and use their hands and use computers, smartphones, and other devices. Amputees will be able to control bionic limbs with their thoughts. A version of this technology may 1 day restore vision to people who are blind.

What else could a brain interface do in the future?

Elon Musk has predicted that Neuralink could potentially eliminate the need for languages, through a universal thought language that allows everyone to communicate via a future version of Neuralink.

We could also see the power of mental telepathy move from science fiction to science reality. Using our minds to communicate is a form of mental telepathy, which is the transmission of information from one person's mind to another. What if anything we think or imagine could be transmitted to any smartphone or laptop in the world? Two or more people could communicate directly using wireless neural links. WE would become the smartphone.

Instead of typing messages on our phones and laptops, we would *thinkchat*. Instead of telling Alexa or Siri or an AI assistant what we want, we could simply think it. The entire Internet and cloud could become extensions of our brain. Students could "learn" by downloading lessons directly to their brains. We could share information like we share documents on email, through brain-to-brain connections that might be called *brainmail*.

Neural implants that allow us to move external devices could also give us a form of telekinesis—the power to move objects with our thoughts. This would unleash incredible powers that previously only existed in science fiction.

Given these possibilities, we should ask: do we really want our minds to be connected to each other, anywhere, anytime? If we develop a way to put our brains online, does that mean our brains could be hacked?

If we can read someone's mind using a computer chip, does that mean we could copy someone's thoughts, memories, emotions, and personality? If we can clone the brain, does that mean we can preserve and replicate the memories and personality of a person? Could the brain be "downloaded" and transferred to a computer or robot? And if so, could the replicant or robot keep learning and developing?

Would this be a way to engineer a type of "immortality" by reading and transferring the brain like we see in science fiction movies?

Of course, copying the contents of someone's brain to a computer is not really immortality since a copy is not the original. If John Smith's brain could be copied and cloned, John's cloned brain would be a copy, but it would not be John. If I copy an original document in a photocopier, the copy is not the original. The same would happen if we copy ourselves, our minds, personalities, memories, experiences, etc., into a computer. The computer version would be a copy, and the COPY might be immortal, but the original would still age and die.

Still, the "value proposition" is intriguing. Imagine being able to preserve and access the wisdom of our greatest thinkers—geniuses as smart as Einstein or Stephen Hawking (or Elon Musk)—preserving the "brainpower" of our smartest innovators, entrepreneurs, scientists, thought leaders, gurus, and philosophers. If we could keep alive the smartest people in the world, we could create a "genius bank" that we could access to help solve future problems.

We should recognize that there are nefarious possibilities to these innovations. For example, neural-linked soldiers could control weapons with their brains. Combat pilots could aim and fire weapons with their thoughts. Research on this is already underway, which is a scary thought.

Elon Musk has warned that a danger of artificial intelligence that "lives forever" might be the creation of dictators who never die. He points out that Hitler was mortal and he died, which is good, but an AI version of an insane dictator like Hitler who could live for centuries or forever would be disastrous.

In reality the likelihood is remote, given that an interface that can read and replicate the entire brain would require preserving and maintaining more than 86 billion neurons with all their complex functions and interactions including processes that are biochemical.

Wearable Computers

Exoskeletons and Exo-Suits

One of the most priority high-value needs that requires more innovation involves exoskeletons and bionic body aids needed to help stroke victims, paraplegics, and amputees. Being able to connect the brain to exoskeletons would restore normal mobility to millions of patients and also reduce the cost of caring for paralysis victims.

What's Needed? A basic need for handicapped patients is a technology that would replace the wheelchair. Robotic exoskeletons have the potential to address this need.

New ways to give more independence and mobility to paralysis victims are desperately needed. Any innovation that gets patients out of wheelchairs and "on their feet" would provide enormous benefits for the entire handicapped community.

Many of the exo-suits that exist today are regulated by control pads. Being able to link exoskeletons and other bionic devices directly to the brain using Neuralink or a similar brain-machine interface would be a major breakthrough. A brain-machine interface for exoskeletons whether it's based on an implanted neurochip or external connection of some sort represents a major advance.

Exoskeletons can cost $100,000 or more, so innovative solutions that reduce the cost and longer-lasting batteries to power the suits are also needed.

What's Possible? Wearable exoskeletons and bionic suits are commercially available from Ekso Bionics and other providers.

Ekso Bionics is a pioneer in powered lower-body and full-body exoskeletons that give mobility to paralysis victims. The EksoNR is a lower-body gait assist exoskeleton approved by the FDA for multiple sclerosis patients.

The first exoskeleton to receive FDA clearance for personal and rehabilitation use is ReWalk™, a wearable exoskeleton developed by ReWalk Robotics that provides powered hip and knee motion to help individuals with spinal cord injuries to stand, walk, turn, and climb stairs. ReWalk is also approved for use in rehabilitation clinics in the European Union.

In January 2023 the FDA approved the use of Atalante, a self-balancing, battery-powered exoskeleton designed to assist rehabilitation of stroke victims. There is a strong need for this technology because every year 795,000 people in the United States suffer strokes. The French manufacturer Wandercraft indicated that Atalante is designed for use in rehabilitation, not for everyday use.

Honda has introduced a hands-free wheelchair called the UNI-ONE that moves like a hover board when the user tilts their body in the direction they want to move.

Lockheed Martin's Human Universal Load Carrier (HULC) is an industrial and combat exoskeleton that gives additional strength to workers and soldiers. This robotic support allows the wearer to carry hundreds of pounds. This adds superhuman strength to workers and allows soldiers to carry heavy weapons. Ottobock, a German prosthetics company, also makes load-handling exoskeletons, shoulder supports, and other wearables.

In the coming decade, the development of lighter, stronger, and flexible nanomaterials that combine plastics and metals will make exoskeletons more affordable and more comfortable for wearers.

Drones

Look, in the Sky, It's a Bird, It's a Plane, It's a...*Drone*!

Drones, also known as unmanned aerial vehicles (UAVs), are robotic aircraft that are controlled remotely or operate autonomously. They come in many different sizes and configurations, from winged aircraft to helicopters and quadrotors. Aerial drones are essentially flying robots and as such are the largest commercial robot application in the world. At the beginning of 2023, according to the FAA, 855,000 aerial drones were registered in the United States.

Drones can go to places that are too remote or too hazardous for humans to reach. They can deliver emergency medical supplies and food to remote areas isolated by floods or earthquakes. They can also be used to take aerial photos of ourselves at work or on vacation.

When the first self-propelled drones were first introduced, they were mostly viewed as toys like model airplanes. Since then, the drone market has become a multibillion-dollar industry. Amazon lists more than two dozen aerial drones for sale. The world's leading drone manufacturer is Da-Jiang Innovations (DJI), based in Shenzhen, China. DJI's annual sales are nearly $4 billion. The company's global market share is estimated at 70%.

One of the earliest and best drone applications is aerial photography. Cameras mounted on drones can cover news events, add an eagle's eye view to films and documentaries, and capture airborne selfies. Flying drones are also to provide information to firefighters, first responders, and rescue teams. Weather drones are used in storm tracking. Farmers use drones to track livestock. Archaeologists use infrared drones to detect ancient cities and monuments hidden in the jungle or desert.

A commercial application that is already being tested and commercialized involves package delivery. Amazon, UPS, and other delivery services have designed autonomous drones that can deliver packages by air, faster, and at lower cost than ground delivery.

In 2019, the Federal Aviation granted UPS Flight Forward the first approval to operate their Prime Air fleet of delivery drones for package delivery. Amazon has also received approval to operate their fleet of Prime Air delivery drones which are designed to deliver packages in 30 min or less.

What's Needed? For many applications, drones need more flying time which means there is a need for drones that can fly longer distances, stay in the air longer, and use less energy. This means we need to develop drones with lighter longer-lasting batteries as well as solar-powered drones.

The primary need for aerial drone innovations, in addition to lower cost and better performance, is to provide aerial functions that are faster and less expensive than ground vehicles, standard helicopters, satellites, and other methods.

For example, an ambulance can take precious minutes or hours to transfer a donor organ from one hospital to another. Aerial drones can deliver donor organs to recipients much faster than an ambulance which may be what's needed to save lives.

In addition to aerial drones, there is a need for better, more efficient seaborne drones that can be used for a variety of purposes on lakes, rivers, and oceans. Imagine a drone that can fly over rough seas to reach a drowning victim, land on the water, and provide a life buoy.

Here's an interesting bit of trivia. The concept for a seaborne drone was actually patented by Nicola Tesla in November 1898! In his patent application, Tesla describes a vessel with no wires, cables, or other electrical or mechanical connection that could be controlled by producing "waves, impulses or radiations which are received through the earth, water or atmosphere by suitable apparatus by suitable apparatus on the moving body and cause the desired actions…" He was talking about controlling drones using radio signals. He also discussed the potential for using drones as weapons of mass destruction.

What's Possible Many experimental enhancements are being tested using aerial drones today. For example, a new generation of ultrawide-band radar is giving drones the ability to see through walls, detect the heartbeats of survivors, and find victims lost in forests or trapped in buildings destroyed by earthquakes or bombs.

In Ukraine, the Mideast, and other combat environments, military drones have demonstrated a potential to become a force multiplier. Military drones have the potential to help smaller fighting units a prevail against larger conventional armies. Combat drones are already providing real-time surveillance and targeting. They can provide precise GPS locations of troop and weapon locations in combat zones. Drones can also carry a wide variety of weapons and explosives.

It's been said that aerial drones as an innovation are "out of this world," and that's literally true. NASA's Mars drone, known as Integrity, arrived on Mars on February 18, 2021. The drone weighs 4 pounds and has a wingspan of 4 ft. By the end of 2023, Integrity had conducted more than 60 aerial flights. The drone's mission was to test aerial flight in the thin Martian atmosphere, as well as to capture aerial images. The Mars drone was developed by a group of creative engineers at NASA JPL.

Autonomous Vehicles

Self-Driving Vehicles Are on the Road

Self-driving vehicles (SDVs) are robotic vehicles that can function autonomously without a driver. When cars, buses, and trucks become fully autonomous, they will change our behavior, our culture, and our concept of transportation. Instead of negotiating streets, roads, and highways to get to work, automated driving will be like having a chauffeur, and the smart vehicle will become a robotic chauffeur. The development of semiautonomous and fully autonomous vehicles is the beginning of an entirely new transportation ecosystem.

Applications for SDVs include commuting to and from work, public transportation, on-demand robotaxis, and transport systems for university campuses, industrial parks, and shopping malls.

Every year in the United States, there are around 40,000 traffic deaths per year which means more than 100 people die every day in traffic accidents. A major value proposition for self-driving cars is to make driving safer because computer-guided cars are less likely to have accidents than humans because they can be programmed to obey all traffic laws. Computers don't try to text while driving, don't experience road rage, don't get careless, and don't drink and drive or fall asleep at the wheel. SDVs are also potentially more fuel efficient.

What's Needed? Before the pandemic, more than 140 million Americans commuted to work every day. Despite the trend to work less in offices and work at home more, millions of people still commute to and from work, spending hours in slow-moving traffic lines.

Self-driving vehicles are ideal commuting vehicles because groups of friends and colleagues can be picked up at their homes and automatically driven to their workplace. They can text during the ride and read or work online during the ride, making them much more productive.

SDVs are also ideal utility vehicles for use in street cleaning and transporting heavy or hazardous materials at a large construction site. They can also travel in war zones and other dangerous places.

Before autonomous vehicles are approved, better navigation and accident avoidance systems are needed. Some SDVs use optical systems to avoid collisions and accidents, but how does an optical system differentiate between a yellow construction barrier, a bush with yellow flowers, or a small child in a yellow raincoat chasing a ball into the road?

One of the earliest SDV fatalities occurred when a vehicle on autopilot could not optically differentiate the side of a gray truck from the gray sky behind it on an overcast day.[4] Another incident involved a car on autopi-

---

[4] Thadani, Trisha et al.; The final 11 seconds of a fatal Tesla Autopilot crash; The Washington Post; 6 October 2023.

lot that thought the picture of a stop sign on a bulletin board was a real stop sign. There are also complications caused by heavy rain, snow, ice, and even swarms of bugs that can block or confuse sensors. What if a spider builds a web across a critical sensor overnight while your car is in the driveway? Ford's self-driving vehicles are equipped with air baffles to keep mud, bugs, or ice from spattering and obscuring sensors, especially at high speeds.

On February 6, 2017, a pickup truck dropped 42 gallons of maple syrup on a highway in Vermont, which temporarily closed the road. How do we program an SDV to recognize and deal with a highway covered with maple syrup?

Smarter sensors and object detection systems are needed to help SDVs detect unexpected encounters such as a person dashing into the street, a bicycle rider veering into a traffic lane, a tree falling during a windstorm, construction blocking a route, detours that reroute traffic, and road construction.

Some SDV systems use a combination of GPS, optical sensors, and LIDAR (low-intensity radar). SDVs with optical sensors maintain large fast access image libraries to help recognize various objects and obstacles. Another solution that has been proposed involves outfitting traffic lights with wireless sensors that an SDV could use to navigate predefined routes. Sensors embedded in "smart highways" are another potential solution.

SDVs also need to be given "ears" so they can recognize the difference between police and ambulance sirens and community tests of emergency sirens. Waymo hosted its first "emergency testing day" in 2017, in partnership with the Chandler, Arizona police, and fire departments. Waymo trained its autonomous Chrysler minivans to detect, recognize, and respond to a variety of emergency sounds. They tested the ability of vehicle sensors to "hear" these sounds at different speeds and distances and used the data to compile of emergency sights and sounds.

One interesting problem involves how a traffic cop issues a ticket if an SDV makes an illegal turn or has a burned out tail light. Does the owner get the ticket, or the passenger, or is the SDV treated as a separate entity?

Most SDVs in the United States are semiautonomous, which means they include driver assist/autopilot features that help drivers stay in their road lanes, maintain safe distances, and automatically brake to avoid collisions. What's needed are fully autonomous vehicles that can drive safely and navigate reliably without a human driver.

Several obstacles need to be addressed by SDV engineers, such as whether fully autonomous vehicles can operate with optical sensors only, with LIDAR systems only, or a combination of optical and LIDAR sensors and how to deal with emergencies such as a detour, an emergency vehicle that needs to pass, construction lane closures, people and animals that might dash in front of the vehicle, and human drivers who make unsafe moves. Ironically, one of the most dangerous threats to autonomous vehicles are human drivers who make sudden moves such as changing lanes without signaling or swerving in front of another vehicle while passing.

Whatever can be done to make autonomous smarter, better able to deal with unexpected situations, and also to provide ways for vehicles to "learn" from traffic experiences and encounters will speed the adoption of fully autonomous vehicles.

The development of fast, low-orbit satellite constellations like Starlink has enabled autonomous vehicles to quickly access databases in the cloud. Speedy cloud access is needed to help identify the vast array of situations, objects, and dangers that a vehicle might encounter that need to be recognized quickly.

Robotaxies like Waymo, Uber, and Lyft are already being deployed in several communities. These fleets require the best possible mapping and navigation systems. Navigation apps like Google Maps gave us a head start so we already know how to do this. We need to make sure that SDV navigation is as good or better as mapping systems used by human drivers.

What's Possible? Fully autonomous SDVs are being tested in many cities and towns around the world and in some cases are already being deployed. Autonomous buses that follow predetermined routes are one of the first commercial applications for SDVs. The first robotaxies are being tested in communities where streets are easy to map and navigate. In China and other countries, hundreds of autonomous street sweepers are already in use, traveling prescribed routes to keep streets clean.

A few carmakers are experimenting with radical innovations to help keep drivers safe such as lane keeping sensors, blind spot detection, collision avoidance, automatic braking systems, video cameras, and automatic parking. Some systems can monitor a driver's face, eyes, and posture to detect if someone is getting drowsy or inattentive. Some of these driver-assist functions are being incorporated into traditional gas-powered vehicles and hybrids.

When autonomous vehicles are fully developed and certified as safe and reliable, it then becomes possible to have "on-demand vehicles" like we have on-demand movies and TV shows. In the future, we might not need to own a car or have a garage. We could summon a car from a central dispatch center and choose from different models depending on our needs. During the week we may use a small commuter car to take us to work, and on the weekend we may get an SUV or minivan to take kids and friends to a soccer game. The on-demand vehicle would arrive at our house, apartment, or office when we need it.

Currently in California where many SDVs are being tested, vehicles can be driven in full autonomous mode but require safety operators ready to disengage the system and grab the steering wheel or hit the brakes if required.

One of the earliest and most successful SDV programs is Waymo, which started as an innovation "skunkworks" at Google (Alphabet). Waymo was spun out from Google in 2016 and began testing SDVs in Florida in September 2019. In 1 year, Waymo reported only one "disengagement" requiring human intervention once every 11,000 miles. In February 2024, Waymo received approval from the California Public Utilities Commission to operate a commercial robotaxi service in Los Angeles, the San Francisco Peninsula, San Francisco Airport, and San Francisco freeways. Waymo is the most successful example of autonomous vehicles used for commercial robotaxis in the United States (Fig. 9.7).

Other automakers that have conducted ambitious SDV pilot programs include Fiat-Chrysler (partnered with Jaguar), GM Cruise, Oxbotica (UK), TuSimple (partnered with UPS), and Daimler Trucks. Samsung has partnered with Hyundai to design SDVs in South Korea.

Fig. 9.7 Waymo's self-driving Chrysler Pacifica Minivan. (Source: WAYMO)

In 2023–2024, several electric vehicle manufacturers cut back or eliminated SDV production due to lagging market demand. Demand for fully electric vehicles was impacted by high retail prices, limited driving range on a battery charge, slow charging in cold weather, the high cost of replacement batteries, and recycling issues. Several Detroit automakers reduced SDV inventories, and rent-a-car fleets such as Hertz reduced their electric car fleet.

In February 2024, Apple's stealth project to develop an autonomous electric car was abruptly abandoned after more than a decade of development work. As many as 1400 employees were terminated or reassigned. Apple's electric car initiative, called Project Titan, was initiated in 2014.

Market demand for electric vehicles will be restored when (1) improved technology provides better battery performance and mileage per charge and (2) the cost of full electric vehicles is reduced. More innovation is needed to improve SDV performance and reduce retail prices. Cost/price solutions may come from low-cost manufacturing centers such as China and India.

China is a major developer of SDVs. In 2021, the Chinese government established 16 autonomous driving demonstration zones and approved more than 3500 km of roads for test driving SDVs. Baidu and Yutong Group, based in Zhengzhou, China, started deploying its Xiaoyu 20 autonomous bus in 2021. The bus incorporates artificial intelligence, sophisticated sensors, 5G and cloud connectivity, and other innovations. Shanghai enacted several measures in 2022 to promote the development and use of self-driving vehicles in the city's Jiading district. Potential applications include public transport (buses and robotaxis), intelligent heavy trucks, sanitation, and delivery vehicles.

Climate Innovation

Slowing and Adapting to Climate Change

Climate change poses a real threat to our planet and to human civilization. We need to find better ways to (1) prevent or minimize climate change and (2) adapt to changes that are inevitable.

I can confirm this because I studied climate change while earning a master's degree in environmental studies from the University of Pennsylvania. My graduate thesis was entitled "The Paradoxes of Global Warming." I can report from my studies that global warming is real and human activity is the primary cause.

When I earned my graduate degree in 2010, the CO_2 level was 390 parts per million. In 2023, CO_2 levels had increased to 420 ppm. We know from research on CO_2 levels in unventilated buildings that people start to complain about the air being "stuffy" when CO_2 levels reach 550 parts per million, so 550 ppm is probably the level when the outside air becomes "stuffy." Scientists currently expect CO_2 levels to reach 550 ppm by 2050. At this rate, we could see a time when outdoor workers need to carry extra oxygen and people with asthma and other respiratory conditions have to spend most of their lives indoors.

What's Needed? When it comes to preventing or slowing climate change, we already know what's needed.

Some things we need to stop. For example, we need to stop saturating the atmosphere with greenhouse gases from burning coal and oil. We need to reduce the use of gas-powered vehicles. We need to stop using materials that pollute air, soil, and water. We need to stop polluting the oceans with waste plastics and chemicals that are killing ocean reef systems.

Many of the technologies needed to make these changes are not yet efficient or cost-effective which means more innovation is needed. For example, the batteries used in electric vehicles are expensive, require a lot of energy to build, and contain hazardous chemicals that make it difficult to recycle or dispose of them. We need to design alternative energy vehicles and batteries that are more efficient and affordable. We need to make our homes, office buildings, and factories more energy efficient by requiring new buildings to be net zero, meaning energy and waste neutral. We need to change most or all product packaging from disposable to recyclable.

Unfortunately, several countries with large populations continue to build and use coal-fired energy plants and gas-powered vehicles. As long as this continues, it will be difficult to stop climate change because climate control won't succeed unless most countries implement what's needed.

If we are unable to stop the practices that are creating climate change, we will be forced to find innovative ways to *adapt* to climate change. This means we'll need to reduce energy use which could require periodic blackouts which is already common in some countries. We may also need to keep using fossil fuels and impose a fee or tax to subsidize the cost of developing more efficient alternative energy solutions. Cities that are at risk of being flooded by rising sea levels may need to build seawalls to prevent flooding. Many cities may need to be abandoned which means we'll need to consider relocating large populations.

If we cannot prevent cities from being inundated by rising sea level, we may need to build floating megacities, contained in huge transparent spheres on stilts that rise and fall with the tides. We may also design floating shopping malls. Floating designs are already being developed by architects, and we're beginning to see some examples of floating buildings. Apple's dome-shaped floating store at the Marina Bay Sands in Singapore is an interesting example (Fig. 9.8).

What's Possible? Engineers are already designing net zero buildings—buildings that produce as much energy as they use and generate net zero waste and water. The goal of net zero buildings is not just to make buildings more resource efficient to save money but also to implement sustainable practices that will slow or stabilize climate change which is needed to save the planet.

An international design system called Leadership in Energy and Environmental Design (LEED) rates green building projects and

Fig. 9.8 Apple's floating store in Singapore provides a glimpse of how coastal cities may adapt to rising sea levels caused by global climate change. (Photo by Roberto Dillon)

provides accreditation to construction professionals. Worldwide, there are more than 185,000 LEED-certified commercial green building projects in the world. In 2018, the mayors of 19 cities in the world pledged to make new and existing buildings carbon neutral by 2030. Many cities now require new construction to be "carbon neutral."

While most conservation solutions focus on pollution on Earth, we should also think about pollution in space. Thousands of pieces of space debris from rocket launches and obsolete satellites are orbiting the planet at approximately 15,000 miles per hour, faster than a speeding bullet, and this space junk poses a hazard to future space launches and missions. We need to find creative and cost-effective ways to clean up this debris and also to prevent space pollution in the future. It is admirable that the thousands of satellites in Elon Musk's Starlink network are comprised of materials that are designed to completely burn up when the satellites are obsolete and fall out of orbit. This is the kind of responsible innovation that is needed in every industry.

If we think in terms of global innovations that could help the entire world, one possibility involves geo-engineering. For example, some scientists have proposed building adjustable shields on Earth or in space that can help shield radiation and heat from the sun like a thermostat controls the climate in our homes and offices. It is ironic that we can control the temperature and humidity in any room in a house, but we can't control the climate or prevent natural disasters like hurricanes and tornadoes.

Another technology that exists today but is not yet economical or efficient enough involves carbon capture, which involves extracting CO_2 from fossil fuel plants and storing the CO_2 (which creates additional challenges) or separating oxygen and carbon which is an ideal solution, although currently too expensive.

In countries such as the United States where fossil fuels are plentiful, the economic benefits and desire for energy independence have pitted climate control advocates against political and commercial interests. Finding common ground is essential to reducing climate change. The ideal solution is to make energy-efficient technologies more affordable, efficient, and commercially viable.

Nano-Innovation

Think Small to Get Big Results

Nanotechnology innovations have given us the ability to manipulate nanoscale atoms and molecules like we use LEGO blocks to build toys. This is a remarkable achievement, given that the nanoscale is a billionth of a meter, smaller than the bandwidth of visible light waves, which means too small to be viewed with optical microscopes. We have to use electron scanning microscopes to view and capture images of nanosized structures and processes.

I happen to have some special expertise in this area. In 2016 I was trying to find a good book on nanotech innovations but couldn't find anything suitable, so I wrote my own book, entitled *Nano-innovation: What Every Manager Needs to Know (Wiley)*. I also served a year on the US Nanotechnology Triennial Review committee which was tasked with evaluating and recommending improvements to the billion-dollar National Nanotechnology Initiative. What I learned from my research is that thinking small can lead to some very big achievements.

Nano-innovators have already produced some amazing results. Nanoscale structures and circuits have made electronic devices smaller, lighter, and faster and enabled computer devices and storage drives to grow from megabytes and gigabytes to terabytes and larger.

Nanomedicine has transformed the field of medicine. Scanning electron microscopes allow researchers to study biological structures and processes that previously couldn't be seen with traditional microscopes. Nano-sizing drug molecules allow cancer drugs to enter and destroy cancer cells. Nanocarriers are being used to transport therapeutic genes, proteins, and messenger RNA (mRNA) directly to cells. Some of these nanocarriers have coatings that prevent the body's immune system from rejecting the carriers or the drugs they contain.

Hundreds of nanomaterials have been engineered by reconfiguring molecules to make them stronger and easier to connect and manufacture. One example is carbon nanotubes, which are tube-shaped carbon molecules. The carbon nanotube market was valued at over $6 billion in 2021 and is expected to exceed $20 billion by 2030. Commercially, carbon nanotubes are often mixed with cement, plastic, or other materials to increase strength and durability.

Another form of carbon called graphene is a super material made from a one-atom-thick layer of carbon atoms arranged in a hexagonal lattice. Physically it looks like chicken wire. Many other nanomaterials are being engineered, and we can expect much more in the near future.

The following impact map describes some of the areas where nanotechnology has the potential to transform industries and markets. Many of these innovations are already being implemented and commercialized (Fig. 9.9).

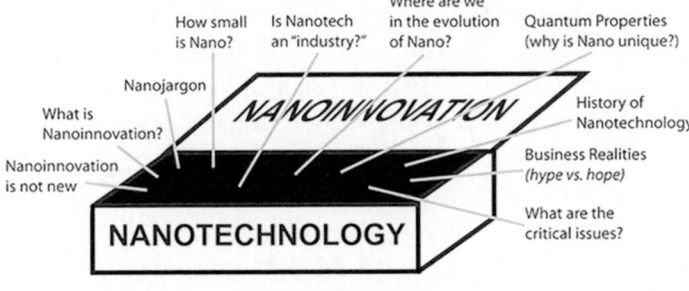

Nano-Imaging
(Imaging of Nanoscale Biological Processes to Understand Disease Related Factors)

NanoMaterials
(Graphene, Aerogels, Carbon Nanotubes, Fullerenes, Metal/Plastic Nanocomposites)

NanoMedicine
(Nano-Sized Drugs, Nanocarriers, Nanobots, Biosensors)

NanoInnovation

What is Nanoinnovation?
Nanoinnovation is not new
Nanojargon
How small is Nano?
Is Nanotech an "industry?"
Where are we in the evolution of Nano?
Quantum Properties (why is Nano unique?)
History of Nanotechnology
Business Realities (hype vs. hope)
What are the critical issues?

NANOTECHNOLOGY

Nanobots
(Molecular-scale Electronics, Sensors, and Motors)

NanoCircuits
(Nanoscale Architectures used in Semiconductors and Computer Circuits)

NanoCoatings
(For spacecraft, clothing, furniture, vehicles etc.)

Fig. 9.9 Nanotechnology gave us the ability to manipulate atoms and molecules and opened a gateway to a plethora of possibilities for a new generation of scientists, engineers, and entrepreneurs. This innovation map shows some of the many "nano" possibilities. (Source: M.Tomczyk)

What's Needed Creating a nanomaterial in a laboratory is easier than ever today; however, the challenge is to find ways to manufacture nanomaterials so they can be used in commercial applications. Graphene has enormous potential, for example, but manufacturing sheets of carbon that are only one atom thick is difficult which is why graphene is only beginning to be used in real-world applications.

Moving nanomedical innovations from the lab to patient has presented a variety of challenges. What's needed are more successful clinical trials and methods for commercializing the use of nanomedicine discoveries and therapies.

What's Possible Nano-innovation has given us access to Ant Man's world which is a fictional world in the movies. In the NeoWorld our ability to innovate at the nanoscale is showing how thinking small can really produce big results.

Being able to manipulate atoms and molecules means that we can combine different types of materials that were previously incompatible. Combining metals and plastics have given us hybrid materials that are literally one atom thick, lightweight, flexible, and stronger than steel or aluminum.

In 2022, a team of chemical engineers at MIT created an entirely new type of plastic called 2DPA-1 that is wafer thin and transparent and provides up to six times more resistance than bulletproof glass. 2DPA-1 is the first two-dimensional polymer sheet that has a smooth surface without bumps. This innovation came from rearranging polymer molecules to connect in flat 2D sheets only one or two atoms thick, which manufacturers previously thought was impossible. Best of all, this material is able to self-assemble and can be affordably manufactured on a large scale.

Nanocircuits and other semiconductor architectures are making it possible for engineers to keep increasing computing power and memory while shrinking the size and profile of electronic devices. Some of the possibilities which are beginning to be commercialized include flexible smartphones and flexible batteries.

Nanomedicine is also beginning to produce extraordinary results. Some researchers believe the next wave of medical innovation will involve the use of nanobots—nanoscale robots—that are programmed to deliver drugs, proteins, and blood cells inside the body. Theoretically, nanobots could be injected into a patient who is susceptible for a specific disease and triggered to activate if and when the disease begins to form.

Neo-Wars

Future Wars Will Be Won with Neo-Weapons

We are definitely moving into a new era of warfare where military forces have access to an arsenal of totally new weapons that include airborne and seaborne drones, GPS-based weapon targeting, and other innovations.

It is becoming clear that the size of a country's army no longer guarantees victory. Military commands that understand technology have a distinct advantage over military forces that rely on the size of their army, air force, and navy. When Russia invaded Ukraine in 2014, their military might and element of surprise allowed them to capture the Crimean peninsula and the eastern region of the country. This was how large nations have seized territory from neighboring countries for thousands of years.

However, when Russia invaded the Ukraine in February 2022, the world was surprised when Ukraine, a smaller mostly agricultural nation, was able to resist and stall the much larger Russian military force. The key to Ukraine's success was smarter use of digital innovation. Ukraine demonstrated how aerial and seaborne drones can be used as force multipliers to stave off a vastly superior enemy force.

Ukrainian forces used aerial drones to locate and pinpoint enemy targets. They used precision-guided artillery to destroy hundreds of tanks as well as troop concentrations, weapons depots, enemy headquarters, and airfields. They hacked enemy phone lines and databases to reveal the location (and morale) of Russian troops and to determine where high-level meetings would be held that could be targeted.

At the beginning of the war, when Russia attempted to disable the nation's communications network to block access to the Internet and GPS, the Ukrainians used alternative Internet networks such as Starlink to maintain military and civilian communications. They also used satellite, GPS, and drone technologies to deploy smart artillery, smart antiaircraft weapons, and antimissile systems. The Ukraine military command reportedly trained as many as 10,000 fighters to operate military drones. In early 2024, the Ukrainian Armed Forces established an Unmanned Systems Forces group.

Ukraine also pioneered the use of seaborne drones and swarms of drones which are difficult to defend against. On April 14, 2022, Ukraine's Bayraktar TB2 drone helped sink the Russian flagship Moskva. Whether the Russia-Ukraine conflict continues for years or decades or not, the use of Neo-War weapons has forever changed the nature of war.

Other innovations in the military space include defensive systems that provide defensive umbrellas, such as Israel's Iron Dome system, which has intercepted hundreds of missiles fired at military and civilian targets.

What's Needed? The most important need for military innovation in the NeoWorld involves the development of lower-cost antimissile umbrellas to defend against enemy rockets, missiles, and drones. These systems need to be refined and expanded to be able to deal with large swarms of drones and rockets that can overwhelm most antimissile batteries.

There is a specific need to defend against "swarm attacks"—barrages that may include hundreds of missiles and rockets—and these systems need to be cost reduced. Israel's Iron Beam is one potential solution, since the cost of firing the laser is only a few dollars per shot compared to thousands of dollars per interception for an Iron Dome missile. It was reported that in 2023, laser defenses were being used to destroy Hamas rockets fired from Gaza and Lebanon.

Military leaders are being forced to ask, will future wars be fought by remote control? Are tanks and trenches becoming obsolete? Should armies, navies, and air forces start developing autonomous (unmanned) versions of aircraft, ships, and fighting vehicles? Do we really need hundreds of thousands of human soldiers to fight and win wars?

What's Possible? In the near future we can expect to see more autonomous weapons including autonomous warships, tanks, mobile artillery, and drones. We may even see robot armies.

The first autonomous robots are already being used in combat. In November 2023, the Israeli military used a semiautonomous robot called Jaguar to clear enemy tunnels in Gaza that were too dangerous for human soldiers to navigate. Jaguar is a six-wheeled robotic vehicle equipped with several sensors including infrared scanning, a machine gun, and other weapons. This weapon provided an innovative approach to clearing dangerous tunnel systems and underground bunkers where enemy soldiers can easily hide, and booby traps are difficult to detect.

Aerial drones are also becoming autonomous. The first known example of an autonomous drone "assassin" was a Turkish autonomous quadrotor called the Kargu-2 that tracked down and attacked human targets in Libya in March 2020.[5]

Seaborne drones for use in oil exploration and restoration of reefs are being tested and deployed in many parts of the world. Underwater drones have the potential to replace submarines which will radically transform naval warfare. A notable example is the Manta Ray seaborne drone being developed by the Defense Advanced Research Projects Agency (DARPA). The Manta Ray comes in several sizes and payload configurations, has the ability to travel long distances, and can hibernate for long periods on the ocean floor without recharging its batteries. Imagine a swarm of hibernating drones being deployed, ready to catch an unsuspecting commercial or military ship off guard. That's a scary but very real possibility.

Drones are also being downsized which is another innovation that will make them difficult to detect and disable. Tiny drones the size of insects are being used to spy and collect information by intelligence agencies. The US Air Force is reportedly testing experimental prototypes of drones that are smaller than insects and may even have wings to help disguise them.

[5] Froelich, Paula; Killer drone 'hunted down a human target' without being told to; New York Post; 29 May 2021.

Space Exploration

Colonizing Mars and Beyond

Elon Musk has announced that he'd like to start colonizing Mars during his lifetime. His goal is to make humanity a multiplanetary species.

NASA is planning to establish a colony on the moon and eventually on Mars, but it is possible that Musk's SpaceX venture may win the race to put humans on Mars.

The colonization of space will be a major benefit to the human race because this is the only way for humanity to survive if an environmental disaster such as a super volcano, asteroid strike, or nuclear conflict devastates the planet.

Most people believe we don't have to worry about leaving the planet to colonize space until the sun dies, billions of years from now. However, the reality is that the geological record shows that extinction events can threaten human civilization any time and often unexpectedly. We are always at risk from potential extinction events which could be triggered by a super-volcano, asteroid collision, nuclear war, or other disaster. This means that as a species, we need to colonize space to ensure our survival because we never know if we have hundreds of years or millions of years of survival on this planet.

Space agencies at many countries have already begun the process of exploring Mars, which is the most habitable planet in our solar system. More than 60 missions have been sent to the Red Planet including seven orbiting spacecraft that have been mapping the surface of the planet and half a dozen rovers that have been landed on Mars. In 2023, two NASA rovers—Curiosity and Perseverance—were actively exploring the surface. These rovers have had to negotiate rough terrain, endure sandstorms, and survive periods of hibernation. Perseverance is accompanied by the Ingenuity drone helicopter. Several countries are collaborating on Mars exploration and can be expected to also collaborate on establishing human colonies.

What's Needed Before Mars can be colonized, a long list of requirements need to be resolved. For example, colonists will need to have efficient spacecraft to transport them safely to Mars, which is 140 million miles from Earth. It takes 80–150 days to travel there.

Despite numerous Mars missions and rovers, we still didn't know what life forms exist there or the effects that low gravity, a thin atmosphere, falling meteors, and solar radiation will have on the first human visitors.

To create a viable community on Mars, human colonists will need reliable sources of air and water, as well as shelter against radiation and sandstorms. Water and ice have been discovered on Mars, but a lot of water is acidic, so cleaner water that can be processed for human drinking needs to be discovered. This critical need will also help determine the best locations to establish the first human colony.

Another need involves finding efficient ways to extract oxygen from the atmosphere which is primarily composed of carbon dioxide.

Human colonies will also need energy to power their habitats, purify water, create breathable air supplies, and provide heat and light. Solar or nuclear power and methane are possible sources of energy. They will need to operate greenhouses to grow food.

Telemedicine will also be an important need for the first colonists, who have to be able to access medical professionals on Earth to help diagnose and treat any illness, especially medical conditions and emergencies such as the effects of radiation or low gravity that may be unique to Mars.

Last but not least, human colonists will need efficient ways to move around Mars which means some sort of vehicle, possibly solar powered or hydrogen powered with a backup battery and self-contained air supply.

What's Possible? Designing a habitable colony on Mars requires an enormous amount of innovation. To get the best ideas and insights, NASA was the first US government agency to develop a formal open innovation process that invites ideas from anyone, anywhere in the world. NASA has solicited ideas for habitat designs and other ideas, with excellent results.

In 2017, NASA issued an open innovation challenge for ideas to program a humanoid robot called Valkyrie to complete repairs on a simulated Mars base. The challenge involved completing a set of tasks on a robot simulator. A total of 93 teams responded, and 20 teams were named finalists. The winner was Kevin Knoedler, an engineer and stay-at-home dad who won $125,000 plus a $50,000 bonus for executing a "perfect run" in the challenge. We can expect to see more open innovation challenges from NASA.

It will also be helpful to collect samples of clay and other materials on Mars and return them to Earth for analysis, for example, to see if surface materials contain water that can be extracted. NASA has collected samples from an asteroid and returned them to Earth, so we know it's possible to collect and return samples from Mars.

One question that lingers is who will be the first Mars explorers? Until recently, the only robots sent to Mars were mechanical rovers. Given the rapid advance in robotics and AI technology, it is now possible to send more sophisticated robots that incorporate generative AI that will act and communicate like real humans and give earthbound scientists advance practice in communicating with Mars colonists. Robots sent to Mars could be humanoids programmed to build habitats with air and water systems before human colonists arrive, so when the first colonies are established, they will already be ready. Having robots build or assemble prefabricated habitats is an efficient way to prepare the planet for human habitation.

Another possibility that is actively discussed in space forums is the concept of terraforming Mars to make all or part of the planet habitable. Mars has a thin dry atmosphere with a week magnetic field which makes the planet generally inhospitable to life. It is possible to create a habitable environment in specific locations such as inside craters or cave systems that could be sustained indefinitely. A longer-term dream is to terraform the entire planet although this could take several lifetimes to complete.

It's important to recognize that there is still a possibility that life exists on Mars in the form of bacteria, insects, or larger species that haven't been discovered yet. The discovery of life on Mars would have significant implications for future explorers and colonists.

Space agencies in several countries and private entrepreneurs are currently working to engineer rockets, spaceships, and habitat designs to create a Mars colony. Both NASA and Musk have suggested that the first human mission to Mars could occur in 2029 or 2030. Elon Musk's SpaceX venture has already developed a super heavy rocket called "Starship" which is a reusable transport system designed to carry crews and cargo to Earth orbit, the moon, and to Mars and beyond. Starship is designed with shields against heat and radiation.

If successful, colonizing space will fulfill the vision of *Star Trek*, the iconic sci-fi series that inspired us to "boldly go where no one has gone before." This is the essence of innovation.

What Comes Next?

From smarter-than-ever humanoids, autonomous cars, and drones
To influencers and social media that glue us to our phones,
These radical opportunities, arriving fast and furious,
Excite our imaginations and make us all so curious
to learn about the future, to innovate and fly,
to test the outer limits and touch the starry sky.
Whoever and wherever we are in life we have an obligation,
To make the world a better place, through Neo-Innovation.

I sincerely hope that this book inspires you to be more creative, more innovative, and better able to navigate changes in the NeoWorld.

Keep going. Do something new. Try a different approach. Solve a problem. Take some risks. Break a rule. Expand your thinking.

Find a way to help improve something in the world, whatever that might be. Find something that's needed, and help make it possible.

The most important thing to keep in mind is that life is a grand adventure…ENJOY!

Wishing you all the best, *Michael S. Tomczyk*

© The Editor(s) (if applicable) and The Author(s), under exclusive license to Springer Nature Switzerland AG 2024
M. S. Tomczyk, *Neo-Innovation*, Business Guides on the Go,
https://doi.org/10.1007/978-3-031-74303-0

Reading List: Innovation Thought Leaders

During my tenure at the Wharton School, I was honored to know and work with many of the leading management researchers and innovation leaders who developed the frameworks used by corporations and government agencies to develop and launch radical innovations. Here is a list of thought leaders and publications that include core concepts for practicing innovation. These books and articles describe some of the most successful best practices and strategies used to develop/launch emerging technologies and applications:

Chesbrough, H. (2003). *Open innovation: The new imperative for creating and profiting from technology.* HBS Press.

Chesbrough, H. (2014). *New frontiers in open innovation.* Oxford.

Christensen, C. (1997). *The innovator's dilemma: When new technologies cause great firms to fail.* Harvard Business School Press.

Christensen, C., & Raynor, M. (2003). *The innovator's solution: Creating and sustaining successful growth.* Harvard Business School Press.

Huston, L., & Sakkab, N. (2006, March). Connect and develop: Inside Procter & Gamble's new model for innovation. *Harvard Business Review.*

Iansiti, M., & Levin, R. (2004, March). Strategy as ecology. *Harvard Business Review, 82*(3).

© The Editor(s) (if applicable) and The Author(s), under exclusive license to Springer Nature Switzerland AG 2024
M. S. Tomczyk, *Neo-Innovation*, Business Guides on the Go,
https://doi.org/10.1007/978-3-031-74303-0

Iansiti, M., & Lakhani, K. (2020, January) *Competing in the age of AI: Strategy and leadership when algorithms and networks run the world*. Harvard Business Review.

McGrath, R., & McMillan, I. (2009). *Discovery-driven growth: A breakthrough process to reduce risk and seize opportunity*. Harvard Business Review Press.

McGrath, R., & McManus. R. (2020) Discovery-driven digital transformation. *Harvard Business Review*.

Prahalad, C. K. (2004, August). *The fortune at the bottom of the pyramid*. Wharton School Publishing.

Schoemaker, P. J. H. (1995, November). Scenario planning: A tool for strategic thinking. *Sloan Management Review*.

Schoemaker, P. J. H., & Tomczyk, M. (2007, January) *The future of biosciences: Four scenarios for 2020 and their implications for human healthcare*. Mack Center/Wharton.

Day, G., & Schoemaker, P. J. H. (2005, November) Scanning the periphery. *Harvard Business Review*.

Tomczyk, M. (2014). *Nano-innovation: What every manager needs to know*. Wiley-VCH.

Tomczyk, M. (2020). Empowering. In *AFTER SHOCK: The world's foremost futurists reflect on 50 years of future shock—and look ahead to the next 50*. John August Media.

Tushman, M., & O'Reilly, C., III. (2004). The ambidextrous organization. *Harvard Business Review*, pp. 74–83.

Bibliography

AKP Staff. (2021, September 10). Social media influencer/model created from artificial intelligence lands 100 sponsorships. *Allkpop*.

Anderson, J., et al. (2021, February 18). *Experts say the 'new normal' in 2025 will be far more tech-driven, presenting more big challenges*. Pew Research Center.

Baig, A., Yee, L., & Singla, A. (2023, January 19). *What are ChatGPT and DALL-E?* McKinsey & Company.

Big Think. (2016, August 23). Nikola tesla predicted drones in 1898. *Technology and Innovation*.

Bremen, J. M. (2024, March 8). Accelerating female innovators. *Forbes*.

Carlson, K. (2024, January 30). Elon Musk's Neuralink, which has Austin offices, just put its first brain chip in a human. *Austin American-Statesman*.

Christensen, C., et al. (2015, December). What is disruptive innovation? *Harvard Business Review*.

Cleveland Clinic. (2021, September 29). 90 percent of heart disease is preventable through healthier diet, regular exercise, and not smoking. *Cleveland Clinic Newsroom*.

Colville, J., & Wolverton, T. (2024, March 8). *Women innovators inspire at 4YFN 2024*. UNDP.

© The Editor(s) (if applicable) and The Author(s), under exclusive license to Springer Nature Switzerland AG 2024
M. S. Tomczyk, *Neo-Innovation*, Business Guides on the Go,
https://doi.org/10.1007/978-3-031-74303-0

Congressional Budget Office. (2023, May 17). *Large constellations of low-altitude satellites: A primer.* U.S. Congress.

Dans, E. (2021, June 3). The pandemic has changed business structures: There's no going back. *Forbes.*

EIT Health. (2024, March 19). *Maria Gonzalez Manso wins 2024 European prize for women innovators.* European Union.

Gangavelli, A., & Morris, A. (2021, October 18). Premature cardiovascular mortality in the United States: Who will protect the most vulnerable among us? *Circulation.*

George, G., Lakhani, K. R., & Puranam, P. (2020, December). What has changed? The impact of COVID pandemic on the technology and innovation management research agenda. *Journal of Management Studies.*

Gerdeman, D. (2021, March). COVID killed the traditional workplace. What should companies do now? *In Practice.*

Hayes, A. (2023, September 29). Smart home: Definition, how they work, pros and cons. *Investopedia.*

Jaurnotte, F., et al. (2023, March 21). How pandemic accelerated digital transformation in advanced economies. *International Monetary Fund/IMF Blog.*

Jukik, S. (2022, December 3). Smartphones have wiped out 97% of the compact camera market. *Shotkit.*

Julia, N. (2023, January 9). *Dementia & Alzheimer's disease statistics and facts (2023 update).* CFAH.

Korosec, K. (2017, December 26). Saudi Arabia's newest citizen is a robot. *Fortune.*

Kurzweil, R. (2006). *The singularity is near: When humans transcend biology.* Penguin Books.

Law, M. (2023, August 10). Top 10 generative AI tools for businesses. *Technology.*

Loftus, Y. (2023, September 20). Autism statistics you need to know in 2023. *Autism Parenting Magazine.*

Lucas, A. (2023, March 5). Nestle, Tyson and other food giants bet on air fryer boom to grow sales. *CNBC.*

McGinn, D. (2020, December 28). What did 2020 do to retail? *Harvard Business Review.*

McKinsey & Company. (2020, October 5). How COVID-19 had pushed companies over the technology tipping point—And transformed business forever. *McKinsey Survey.*

Medium.com. (2020, February 7). *Devoted to discovery: Seven women who have shaped our world.* UN Women.

Mills, C. (2023, July 31). The largest drone companies in the world, and what they do. *HistoryComputer*.

National Institutes of Health. (2020, July 31). *Cognitive super agers defy typical age-related decline in brainpower*. National Institute on Aging.

Newman, A. A. (2023, April 26). How air fryers got so hot. *Retail Brew*.

NSGA Administration. (2015, June 30). *68 is the new 40?* National Senior Games Association Press Release.

Ortiz, P. (2023, September 24). Who invented the air fryer and when? History, present and tips. *House Grail*.

Paulin, M. (2021, October, 7). The effect of technology: How tech has evolved due to the pandemic. *LinkedIn*.

PMR. (2022, May 3). Biggest innovations in plastic 2022. *Plastics Manufacturing Resources*. Queensland Government; 16 April 2018.

Robertson, R. (2023, July 20). Why people in "blue zones" live longer than the rest of the world. *Healthline*.

Rowan University. (2023, September 29). Researchers find link between plastic additive and autism, ADHD. *Rowan Today*.

Roychoudhury, M. (2022, September 12). *World malaria report 2022: The board did not tip, but the storm is not over*. IS Global.

Sauer, M. (2023, April 19). Elon musk now says he wants to create a ChatGPT competitor to avoid 'A.I. Dystopia'—he's calling it 'TruthGPT'. *MakeIt*.

Saunokonoko, M. (2021, June 23). Tiny drones with fluttering wings developed by US Air Force. *9News*.

Smith, J. (2023, September 11). Atezolizumab plus chemo may provide lasting benefit in ES-SCLC. *Cancer Therapy Advisor*.

Tangermann, V. (2023, July 19). Fully AI-generated influencers are getting thousands of reactions per thirst trap. *Futurism*.

Thomas, S. A., Browning, C. J., Charchar, F. J., Klein, B., Ory, M. G., Bowden-Jones, H., & Chamberlain, S. R. (2023, October 13). Transforming global approaches to chronic disease prevention and management across the lifespan: Integrating genomics, behavior change, and digital health solutions. *Frontiers in Public Health*.

Trew, J. (2023, July 21). Digital 'immortality' is coming and we're not ready for it. *Engadget*.

Tuquero, L. (2023, October 19). Did Israel use its laser weapon 'iron beam' for the first time? Here's how we know. *Politifact*.

Tyson, N. d G. (2015, March 22). The future of humanity with Elon musk. *Startalk podcast*.

United Nations. (2021, May 3). Global e-commerce jumps to $26.7 trillion, fueled by COVID-19. *United Nations News.*

Upham, B. (2023, March 13). Could the diabetes drug metformin slow the aging process? *Everyday Health.*

Vyas, K. (2023, April 18). A brief history of drones: From pilotless balloons to roaming killers. *Interesting Engineering.*

Wang, L. (2023, October 20). *Trial results confirm effectiveness of atezolizumab against a rare sarcoma.* National Cancer Institute.

Weitzman, C. (2023, May 10). *Embrace the future: How to become an influencer.* Speechify.

Wellcome. (2023, October 3). *Advances in fighting malaria: From bed nets to the first-ever vaccine.* Wellcome.

Worldwide Cancer Research. (2021, March 18). *Why haven't we cured cancer yet?* Worldwide Cancer Research.

Young, J. (2023, March 15). Special purpose acquisition company (SPAC) explained: Examples and risks. *Investopedia.*